A Pie

A Pied Cloak

Memoirs of a Colonial Police Officer
(Special Branch)

Kenya, 1953–66
Bahrain, 1967–71
Lesotho, 1971–75
Botswana, 1976–81

DEREK PETER FRANKLIN, MBE

JANUS PUBLISHING COMPANY
London, England

First published in Great Britain 1996
by Janus Publishing Company
Edinburgh House, 19 Nassau Street
London W1N 7RE

British Library Cataloguing-in-Publication Data.
A catalogue record for this book is available from the British Library.

ISBN 1 85756 294 1

Cover design Harold King

Photosetting by Keyboard Services, Luton, Beds
Printed and bound in England by
Intype London Ltd

To my colleagues
particularly to those who gave their lives
to the maintenance of law and order

DPF Ashford, Kent 1996

Contents

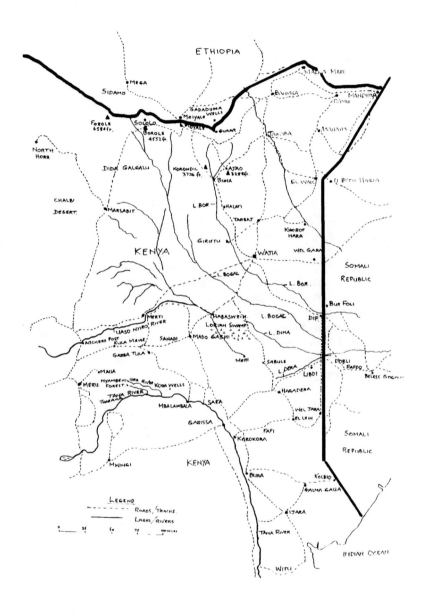

ONE

PSEUDO GANG OPERATIONS AGAINST THE *SHIFTA* IN NORTH-EAST KENYA

We crossed Kenya's north-eastern border into the Somali Republic at 0200 hours, in an area where the border demarcation was a dusty and almost indeterminable cutline in the desert scrub. There was some moonlight and visibility was good, so we avoided established tracks that had been created by both tribal stock and game and, keeping up a comfortable sloping gait, we shuffled along in our open-toed sandals, pausing only when we heard an unfamiliar noise that might threaten the safety of our clandestine mission: to attack a Somali *Shifta* group in what they had come to regard as the safety of their own territory.

Our group was twenty-five in number and consisted of dissident Somalis led by myself, a serving Kenya Police Special Branch Inspector. After one or two minor scares caused by the sudden take-off of a whirring nightjar or the inquisitive snuffling of a hyena, we reached our target: a Somali village some three to four miles from the Kenya border which our own intelligence reports had pin-pointed as a base for a gang of twenty to thirty Shifta who had been responsible for carrying out a whole series of raids against both civilian and security forces personnel.

The Shifta tended to be indiscriminate in their targets, attacking trading stores run by their own tribesmen in addition to those of Asian and Arabs. Vehicles carrying provisions were ambushed and robbed and their occupants terrorised, abducted and killed. Nearer the sanctity of the Somali border, they took pot-shots at our border posts and also fired a number of grenades into the police border post compounds, usually of the Italian Oto Model ·35 type, nicknamed the 'Red Devil'; a grenade that was more threatening to the ear drums than to life and limb.

As we made our muffled approach, a number of things were occupying my mind. The major problem was the wisdom, or lack of it, in a Kenya police officer being the wrong side of the border leading a band of irregulars, all heavily armed and up to no good. Supposing I was wounded, captured or deserted by my men? I knew that capture by the *Shifta* would almost certainly result in an unpleasant end, for I had seen their work at first hand and remembered in particular the death of Ken Arnold, a District Officer from Mandera, and a former Kenya police officer, who had been ambushed by *Shifta*, separated from his *dubas* (Somali tribal police) escort and killed. If I had had any serious doubts about my men's loyalty, then I would not have embarked on the Pseudo Gang assignment. But one has to be realistic: after all the Pseudos were all Muslims; we were in a predominantly Muslim area; and here I was, a 'Nazarine'.

The smell of smoke and the low murmur of voices brought me back to a higher state of alertness, and I was conscious that the sweat that was running down my back was now icy cold, and that I was more frightened than I would ever admit.

It was fortunate for us that the Somalis were grouped around a fire between us and their village. Although as Muslims they consider dogs unclean, largely because of their aptitude for licking parts that others cannot reach, most Somali villages were in fact home to many pye-dogs, usually all skin and bone, but capable of barking at the slightest sound. We were lucky as there were no dogs present. The excitement at being so close and yet undetected increased the rate of my heart beat and dark beads of sweat from my darkened face dripped down my chin. We were close enough now to see and hear that the group around the fire were heavily armed. My nearest Somali whispered in my ear that the group were discussing a recent raid that they had made on a Kenya border post. Three of us crawled closer and I was inwardly praying that no one would break a twig, or put their outstretched hands on a scorpion. My heart, pulse and every other monitorable organ were now working overtime; while I sought to think rationally, the hunter's instinct for a good kill tended to override all other considerations.

It came as an anti-climax when my closest companion put his moist lips against my ear and whispered, 'Mulla.' It would seem that there was a holy man with the *Shifta*, and that he was reading extracts from the Koran to a group of them. By now it was possible to see the armed *Shifta*, perhaps thirty in number, and most of them carrying either a gun or spear, as they chatted amongst themselves, some drinking from gourds, others cleaning their weapons with just a few listening to the words of the mulla. I could clearly see a group of whom I had intended to hit once the balloon went up.

All this had now changed. As my rapport with my colleagues depended largely on mutual respect, there was no way I could ask them to open fire on the *Shifta* with a holy man present. It was true that they had each made a commitment to me to assist in trying to eradicate the terrorism of *Shifta*; but they were all Muslims and it would be dangerous to test their loyalty too far. So we waited. Little did the *Shifta* know how close to death they were; it seemed most unlikely that we would ever again get such a golden opportunity to hit them with so much surprise, but we had to sit it out. I wondered whether my team knew the holy man for, being a largely nomadic race to whom international boundaries were often an inconvenience as they migrated following the rains and better grazing, it was possible that they did and that they had identified his voice.

We lay in extended ambush for about half an hour listening to them talking, spitting and passing round sticks of *ghat*, a stimulant that is in common usage by Somalis and is more usually called *miraa* in Kenya. The build-up of sweat had now started to dry on me and the urge to itch was terrific. Keeping abnormally still creates cramp and there was also the temptation to put one's mind into neutral and doze off. I reminded myself to remain alert, for my colleagues would be quick to notice any indecision or other weakness. It was beginning to get chilly and about time, I thought, that all Holy Men were in bed.

I felt a hand on my knee and young Mohammed, who had been with me from the start, whispered in a my ear that it seemed the mulla was departing for the village. Even I could hear the salutations as a lone figure got up and slouched off into the darkness on the far side. As the fire flickered it was possible to see the crouched figures around the fire and it looked as if a few were settling down to sleep where they were.

By a pre-arranged plan, we split into small groups of about five and, spaced some ten yards apart, we walked into the *Shifta* camp in a rough line abreast. There was no thorn *zariba*, just a few thorn-trees that stabbed us as we brushed through them. I commenced firing when the first *Shifta* voice queried who was approaching. It could only have been at a distance of ten yards or so when I emptied almost a full magazine from my Sterling SMG. This was the signal for the others to open fire with ·303 rifles; a few shotguns plus a sprinkling of ·36 grenades.

In my Mau Mau days we used to call such attacks the controlled rush. In truth it was seldom controlled but had plenty of rush with fingers hastily leaving the trigger as one of your own passed across your line of fire. The great advantage was the speed with which the enemy was attacked, often in thick bush, and the encirclement to his rear that helped to mop up stragglers. On this occasion the attack was a frantic one: the shotgun, rifle fire and bursts of sub-machine-gun fire interspersed with the loud bang of exploding ·36 grenades. There was dust everywhere and this, along with the smell of cordite, filled the nostrils. There was a lot of confusion as we sought to remain in contact with each other, and men were recalled who were keen on pursuit of the now fleeing *Shifta*. We stumbled across bodies and found some items of uniform; but no arms, which pointed to the likelihood that members of the Somali Gendarmerie were with the *Shifta*. Bursts of LMG tracer winged around us as the *Shifta* and company attempted a half-hearted counter attack.

We had stopped firing and the only shots being fired were those of the *Shifta*, who by now were also using rifles and what we later discovered to be Chinese copies of the ·5 Thompson sub-machine-gun. It was also discovered that the ·303 rifles used by the marauding gangs at that time, bore numbers in white paint on their stocks indicating their position in an armoury rack! One suspected that they were left over from colonial days and that they had been handed over to the *Shifta* by the Somali authorities.

By now we were in a heightened state of excitement and my inner voice urged the need for caution. Sensing that we had achieved our aim of scaring the life out of the *Shifta* on their home territory, inflicted serious casualties and dented their *heshima* (pride), I blew my whistle to signal that we break off and return across the border.

As we grouped together trying to identify who was missing and whipping in the odd straggler, I was aware of a curling string of tracer bullets arcing towards us. There was a sudden blow on my hip that made me stumble. It was over in a trice and I only felt bruised but it did help to concentrate my mind on getting the patrol back across the border. We were some ten in number with the remainder, I was told, already ahead of us enroute to the border. We moved off in some haste and were soon safely inside the Kolbio police post, entry to which was gained first by the firing of a Verey pistol, then advancing slowly to be recognised by the General Service Unit (GSU), who had taken over the manning of police posts along the Somali border.

The only discordant note was that the first group to arrive had signalled their safe return to the Provincial Special Branch Officer, Dougie Hughes in Garissa, and he was quite naturally feeling rather shaken. He later told me that he felt physically sick, as he thought that the second group had come a cropper. It was a great boost to our morale to find that we had not incurred any casualties and that from our point of view the operation had gone well. When there was time I checked my bruised hip and found that one of the three magazines in my hip-bandolier had been hit by a bullet which had dislodged several rounds and dented the magazine beyond repair.

When reporting next day to the Provincial Police Commander Superintendent, Murdoch McKenzie, he seemed most impressed, as did Dougie Hughes, and both gave me their full support in the pursuit of my Pseudo team work. It was arranged for another Special Branch Inspector to be posted in to handle the routine work, leaving me free to do other things. Many years later in another world, I was to read the CV of the relieving Inspector and noted with some pride that he had recorded his time in Garissa as being an administrative officer to a Pseudo Gang.

Murdoch McKenzie wrote an extremely commendatory letter to the Commissioner of Police which he let me read. It contained many warming sentiments and it was indeed unfortunate that one of his recommendations, that I should be advanced half a dozen notches up the pay scale, fell on deaf ears. It would certainly have caused a sensation amongst my colleagues. Some of the points advanced in the letter were acted upon and, in due course, things got moving.

As a group we had carried out several other operations prior to this particular cross-border foray, some internally and others against Shifta camps in the Somali Republic. On the first cross-border raid we had waited patiently for a coded signal from Special Branch Headquarters, giving us the necessary clearance, just in case there were any diplomatic talks taking place between the Kenya and Somali governments; but on subsequent raids we went ahead and did not wait for individual clearances.

It had all begun in October 1963 when I was posted from the Special Branch surveillance team in Nairobi to command the Special Branch post at Garissa. Kenya was to become a fully independent member of the Commonwealth on the 12th December after six months of internal self-government and it was deemed politic not to have too many white faces in Nairobi Special Branch at the change-over date; although, strangely enough, the following year I was back there once more with my Kenya colleague William Kivuvani. So on this occasion, leaving William to do the 'eye-balling', I transferred my bachelor person up the dusty road to Garissa.

This was not my first time in the Frontier territory, as I had previously served as District Special Branch Officer at Moyale and Wajir and, from the latter post, I had also had responsibility for Mandera. After a swift settling-in process, one became quickly immersed again in the machinations of the various Somali clans, all of whom were voicing their misgivings at being ruled by 'Black Africans', whom the Somalis considered to be without either religion or culture.

The North-eastern section of the Northern Frontier is peopled largely by Somalis, a hardy pastoral tribe who tend their flocks of camels, cattle and *shoats* (a term that embraces both sheep and goats), moving with the rains and availability of grazing in an area not noted for an abundance of either. Getting into conversation with Somali tribesmen, one soon became aware that they are an intelligent and largely handsome race, quick to anger and slow to forget an insult. They are also politically aware and very proud of their culture. Living in a part of the country where hardship was an everyday feature, they could also be very cruel: they would not hesitate to emasculate or inflict some other equally horrendous mutilation on those enemies that they had shot or knifed whether the person was dead or not; if the enemy were a non-Somali, it would be done instinctively.

I had half a dozen Somali other ranks with which to monitor the political, tribal and cross-border affairs of the local population, with an eye open mainly for the subversive or potentially subversive group or individual. There were local security meetings to attend and liaison meetings maintained with the Kenya Army. My home was a very basic brick building of minute proportions with a galvanised iron roof and no ceiling; consequently during the *jilaal* (hot season), it became so hot in the house that I ate and slept in the dirt surround that was the garden. I did have a source of fresh meat, for I had inherited Dougie Hughes' liking for muscovy ducks and I had acquired a starter flock from him which gave me a plentiful supply of table ducklings, although I did lose several to prowling cobras.

It would have been difficult for me to have made any sort of worthwhile progress in Garissa had I not had the stalwart assistance of Sub-Inspector Baramadei, a Bajun from the Lamu area. He had been my number two in Wajir where his loyalty and diligence, often in the face of Somali belligerence, had been excellent. I was able to pull a few strings and get Baramadei posted to Garissa, accompanied by his Somali wife with whom he lived on and off, usually due to the tribal pressures brought to bear on her.

As the anti-Kenya rumbles from the local population became more pronounced, there was increased talk of armed insurrection as the Somalis saw the day of African rule approaching. They did not want Kikuyu or other Black Africans to be appointed as District Commissioners and Police Superintendents. They could tolerate expatriates; but black infidels was another matter. Rumours of armed gangs crossing over from Somaliland and talk of attacks to be made on Government outposts and individuals was widespread. As a precautionary measure it was recommended, and quickly approved, that the majority of the Somali police officers and their families should be posted down country to Kenya. In a short while a RAF Beverley transport plane took off from the dirt strip at Garissa laden down with the Somali police officers and their kin, and it was quite something to see the RAF crew diplomatically trying to tell the Somalis that their favourite goat could not make the flight as well. The removal of the bulk of the Somalis did assist in ruling out the chances of coercion and perhaps deliberate acts of disloyalty; but it also removed local expertise, some of which it might have been possible to tap. But then one couldn't have it both ways.

The collection of reliable information on the movement of armed Somalis, known as *Shifta* (armed bands of cross-border raiders, whether Somali or Galubba from Ethiopia, have traditionally been known as *Shifta* in the Northern Frontier) was difficult as the Somali population tended to close ranks and were loath to pass on any details to those persons connected with Government. To collect information personally, I had to resort to using Arabs or Asians to act as cut-outs in talking to those Somalis who were likely to know anything of interest. Baramadei had better access, and of an evening he drifted amongst those who were longing to tell someone what they had learnt. There are always those that like to boast, to show they are not afraid to talk about their own people (as long as it is not in public); and he took full advantage of this in addition to lending a sympathetic ear to those whom the *Shifta* had abused by stealing food or physically roughing them up.

By analysing the reports received from various sources and agents, it seemed apparent that a lot of our intelligence was coming from the same or similar sub-source. By a process of elimination it was proved to our satisfaction that some of the more reliable information on armed *Shifta* had its origins in the Somali women who brought milk (from goats, camels and cows) into Garissa market each day from the surrounding *manyattas*. This was where we needed to concentrate our resources, possibly also saving time and money in the process.

Faced with growing evidence of unlawfulness, the Kenya government declared a state of emergency in the Northern Frontier, which gave the security forces a number of additional powers including the right to search offices, stores and houses when there was evidence of an act, or omission, that was likely to have security implications. These wide-ranging powers which included the imposition of curfews, were a great help and were almost immediately used when Special Branch carried out a raid on the local office of the Northern Province Peoples' Progressive Party (NPPPP) – a largely ineffectual organisation whose constitution and clumsy name were masterminded by a couple of expatriates, including the late Ted Casey of Special Branch. The raid was over in a couple of hours, once we had obtained a full list of members and purloined some of their stationery. The office was sealed whilst the membership list was copied, a laborious task as we had no technical facilities in Garissa where pressure lamps and paraffin fridges were de rigeur. The keys were returned to the local Secretary the next day. The raid had an unexpected bonus in that the local office bearers took off for other parts and the NPPPP ceased to function during the remainder of my stay in Garissa.

From elsewhere a list of all Government pensioners resident in the NFD was acquired. This assorted take gave us additional lines for exploitation and was supplemented by assistance from liaison talks with Heads of other government departments, including Dave McCabe, GM, the local Game Scout, who had himself taken a prominent role in anti Mau Mau operations.

Meanwhile, back at the market, the Somali women continued to bring in their gourds and small churns of milk, whilst Baramadei sought an avenue of access. To the best of my knowledge, there were no female police officers serving in the Frontier and, if there had been, they would almost certainly be from a 'down country' tribe and have as much chance as I would, professionally speaking, of making any headway with the Somali women. Observation of the market showed that a young Somali male had a tryst with one of the younger girls and it was thought that he might be approachable. He was what the South Africans would call a *skellam* (a rogue). About 20 years of age, he smoked black *kariko* cigarettes all day, gambled and never seemed to do any work, and was without kin. Young Mohammed was cultivated, found to be receptive and eventually reeled in by Baramadei who weaned him off the card games, drinking and loafing around. Other lines of enquiry also showed promise and we began to get a much better picture of what was going on in the local *Shifta* world.

At that time most of the gangs were crossing into Kenya from Somalia, carrying out raids on the many soft targets available and then high-tailing it back across the border. Later on there was a discernible change as the gangs grew more confident, with groups of twenty to thirty *Shifta* roaming around the Frontier, living off the local population and sometimes banding together to form gangs of 200 strong, when they would take on a police post or a large convoy of traders vehicles that had a large escort from the security forces. Amongst the *Shifta* would be deserters from the Kenya security forces, all of whom would be Somali or part Somali by birth, and elements from the Somali Army or Gendarmerie, who came across the border for some excitement to join their Frontier colleagues in some blood-letting.

The Somali tribes, who along with the Rendille and the Boran were formerly known as Hamitic and now are classified as being Cushitic, have an overall plan to form a Greater Somalia. This would be achieved by the liberation of the Northern Frontier of Kenya and the Ogaden province of Ethiopia, combining them with the former territories of Italian and British Somalilands which had gained their independence in 1960. The five-pointed star that appears on the flag of the Somali Republic refers to those four areas plus the territory of Djibouti, which also seems beyond their grasp. The great complexity of the Somali puzzle goes back to the Berlin conference of 1884 when the European powers carved up the territory in a series of treaties. In the mid-1940s, the Somali Youth League (SYL), began to clamour for a Greater Somalia. In 1950, Britain proposed to the United Nations that for ethnic uniformity the Somali territories be re-united, but this was opposed by the Soviet Union.

Mohammed now started to fulfil what we had suspected he was really capable of. He visited his lady friend at her manyatta (often returning with the milk!) and he seemed to be accepted by her family and, more importantly, the *Shifta* that he came into close contact with. He provided details of gang strengths, weapons and general gossip. He in turn ran small errands for them, thus providing opportunity for contact with his handler. All the *Shifta* gangs that Mohammed met at that time were unknown to us and we suspected that they originated from further north. The *Shifta* were armed mainly with ·303 rifles and the Italian 'Red Devil' grenade; the AK-47s (Kalashnikovs), Siminovs and rocket-propelled grenades came later.

One morning Mohammed turned up with a bandoleer of ·303 ammunition that he had borrowed from a gang. We were worried about him taking such a liberty; but he shrugged it off with his usual 'Ilhumdililie' (By the Grace of God). We took note of the ammunition markings for tracing purposes before pressing him to return the bandolier, so that he did not incur the wrath of the *Shifta*. (The ·303 markings were later confirmed to be consistent with ammunition supplied to British Somaliland prior to independence.) A few days later we heard that a *Shifta* gang had killed a young Somali some ten miles north of Garissa. Fearing the worst, Baramadei and myself with a few armed askaris, drove across country to a small manyatta where we found Mohammed just this side of death's door. He was a bloody mess, having had his wrists and ankles slashed and a bullet put through his throat. On the bumpy ride back to Garissa Mohammed, who had lost a lot of blood and was badly dehydrated had moments of lucidity when he would murmur, 'Silei, silei' (torture, torture). The speed of our Land Rover had to be slow otherwise there was a danger of him being subjected to additional harm. The RAF were contacted to arrange a 'Casvac', and they flew young Mohammed off to Nairobi, with the efficiency and care that one had come to accept, to receive expert medical attention after he had received what must have been life-saving first aid from the local hospital in Garissa.

Some four weeks later Mohammed flew back into Garissa in an exuberant mood, scars the only visible signs of his ordeal. It was clear that he could not take up where he had left off, and that there was no way he could resume his original role and, since he wanted revenge on the *Shifta*, he became the first member of the Pseudo Team that I had been toying with forming. New recruits followed and in a few weeks we had twenty-four Somalis, all of whom were from a sub-section of the Herti who, whilst they might sympathise with the concept of a Greater Somalia, had no time for the terrorism that was being practised by the *Shifta*. Murders of the chiefs and government officials plus the never-ending attacks and pillaging of trading stores had resulted in trading vehicles having to travel in convoys with armed escorts. This was unacceptable to them and they wanted the chance to hit back.

Around the main environs of Garissa, the Provincial Administration had erected a high-wire fence to safeguard the town centre, government offices and living quarters. The enclosed area was known as 'Windsor Park'. There was no Royal connotation as it merely referred to the individual who authorised its construction. Some two miles outside the fence was a collection of deserted brick buildings that in the recent past had been a TB hospital. After discussing the matter with Dougie Hughes, I moved into the buildings with my Somalis, and two Wakamba *askaris* who were both drivers and proficient in small-arms instruction. We began to make the place livable. Defensive sangars and weapons pits were constructed; and some large thorn trees cut down and dragged around the perimeter with the trunks facing inwards so that they formed a formidable thorn *zariba*. There was no water on the site so use was made of a water bowser which was parked centrally so that all could help themselves.

I had acquired an odd assortment of weapons, mainly MK4

·303s, and my two Wakamba got to work instructing the potential Pseudos in their use and maintenance. At that stage we had two Brens for camp defence, later increased to four. The men took well to their instruction and even in their leisure hours could be seen stripping down their weapons and familiarising themselves with firing and loading. The men were fit and wiry with the oldest being in his mid-30s but I did notice that their upper arm development was poor; they might have difficulty in carrying a rifle for a long time, for the use of slings would be prohibited, unless we took something really heavy with us, such as a Bren.

The training went well and even the PT was accepted in good heart. The men were fed, clothed and paid from funds. Some opted to wear the traditional Somali *chuka* or *kikoi* (a sarong-like garment worn round the waist); others wore khaki trousers and shirts that were readily available in local trading stores. This was a good mixture, being one that would match the dress of the *Shifta* gangs whom we would be attempting to impersonate. From the onset it was decided that discipline would be administered by the two eldest Somalis with minor assistance from myself and Mohammed. The system worked well and there were no serious breaches of discipline or security. Anyone wanting to visit his home manyatta had to request permission from his elders. They were aware of the need for discretion and were provided with cover stories to account for their absence from home. Nevertheless, one to had to be realistic, and I did not expect the cover story (a training camp for security guards on the Windsor Park fence) to remain watertight for long.

It was time to test the Pseudos' mettle. Six men were selected, armed with ·36 grenades and driven to an isolated spot on the Somali border some twenty-five miles north-west of Kolbio, where a large *Shifta* camp was known to be sited about five miles into Somalia. I was accompanied by the faithful Baramadei whose normal duties were to collate the workings of the SB office. The group were put over the border early one afternoon in an area of extremely thick bush which; it was hoped, would give the party good cover – both ways. Baramadei and I would wait until midnight for the group to return. If they had not returned by then we would pull out and return to the same point the next morning. Because the Kenya Army were operating along the border further north, the group opted not to take any other weapons other that the grenades.

Once they had vanished into the bush, Baramadei and I moved our Land Rover and ourselves to a fresh position where we could watch the rendezvous point through binoculars. The vehicle was covered in brush and we sat back and waited. Some two to three hours later we heard a series of rolling, muffled explosions and we guessed that the group had thrown at least six grenades. By midnight they had not returned. We ventured on foot to the rendezvous point on several occasions; the moonlight played tricks with our eyes and bushes became people, but to no avail. We pulled out and returned, very cautiously, the following morning but there was no sign of the group and we wondered whether they had in fact been captured or perhaps worse...

The following afternoon we received a radio signal from the Kenya Army to say that our men had walked into the army camp unarmed and exhausted. Along with Superintendent Tony Ryan of Special Branch, I drove to the army camp and collected six very exhausted men. On the way back to camp they excitedly recounted how they had each lobbed two grenades into a *Shifta* camp, in which they could see many men lounging around on the ground under small thorn trees. They said that the grenade explosions threw up clouds of dust, that they could hear screams of pain and, more alarmingly, the *Shifta* pouring out of the camp through several exits in the thorn enclosure in hot pursuit of their attackers. The latter sped away at top speed and, in their enthusiasm to escape, found themselves running away from the border into the Somali interior. They were able to stay together and eventually made a detour back towards the Kenya border which they crossed at a place much further north than their starting point. Not wanting to approach the army camp carrying the remaining grenades, they had buried them and approached the sentry with great caution. Fortunately the Duty Officer knew of the group's role and they were allowed into the camp and afforded hospitality and assistance. The buried grenades were collected later for another venture. The conclusion, based on the group's own individual stories and intelligence reports received in the weeks ahead, was that casualties had been inflicted on the *Shifta* on their home ground, and that no more would they regard their bases as a haven for rest.

Tony Ryan, an officer with some special forces training, I believe in the SAS (TA), suggested that we might like to consider using a 'Q' vehicle, perhaps disguised as a trader's lorry, with a host of armed men inside who could drive the lonely frontier tracks waiting for a gang to jump them. It was a useful suggestion; but I decided against the idea as it would be very difficult to maintain the high degree of secrecy needed, particularly as we had started slinging grenades around. I gather that someone did use this idea later on, but that the *Shifta* never reacted to the trailing cape.

With reports submitted to Nairobi by Superintendents Hughes and McKenzie, the news of the Pseudo operations reached the ears of the Commissioner of Police who signalled his intention to visit our camp. A date was soon arranged and Sir Richard Catling, a man whom I had never met face to face, duly flew into Garissa and then motored into the camp with attendant 'brass', both local and from the capital city. On seeing the wiry Somalis, the Commissioner's first move was to go and feel their arm muscles. We were both impressed: the Commissioner by the strength of their upper arms, and me by his astuteness. I had forgotten that he had served in both the Malayan and Palestine police forces, and that he had considerable experience of unconventional operations. We had a detailed talk, just the two of us tête-à-tête. The Commissioner asking me what exactly I hoped to achieve and what, if anything, I required. I requested a good selection of untraceable firearms plus ammunition, some booby-trapped items, barbed wire and picket posts and an assurance that the funds to feed, cloth and pay my men could continue to be paid from Special Branch funds. Sir Richard assured me that there would be no problems with any of the points that I had raised and we shook hands before he departed back to Nairobi.

This now gave official recognition to what up to that moment had been an enthusiastic local venture.

Within one week an RAF Beverley landed at Garissa with a cargo of barbed wire, six-foot picket posts and sundry other items, mainly for use in camp defence. A week or so later, a courier arrived from Special Branch Headquarters, Nairobi, in an Airwing Cessna, carrying a load of excellent sporting rifles that were in pristine condition plus an abundance of ammunition. All the weapons had had their identification numbers erased. I gathered that the weapons had come from the huge arms depot at Gilgil, which housed something in the region of 250,000 weapons handed in or confiscated during the Mau Mau emergency.

A week or so later, another courier arrived from SB HQ with a smaller but more deadly cargo. This was the booby-trapped equipment arranged for me by Senior Superintendent Bernard Ruck, GM.

The first item was bullets that would explode in the rifle when the gun was fired, the cordite had been removed from the bullets and substituted by something more deadly. We carried out some experiments with the bullets on some seized weapons using a vice and a long (very long!) piece of string. The effect was devastating: the breech of the rifle being blown open, leaving one in no doubt what would happen to the firer. As all and sundry pick up ammunition, including members of the security forces and local tribesmen, the latter having a wide variety of illegal arms, it was considered that such booby trapped ammunition would be too dangerous, so it was returned for destruction. The other item, booby-trapped ·36 Grenades, were another matter and I could see a use for them, albeit under my own strict control.

Our base camp was now ringed by two lines of defence. There was an outer six-foot high barbed-wire fence and then a most formidable zariba of thorn trees that would be a nightmare to anything smaller than an elephant. There would be good lines of fire for the four Bren guns as a large strip of land was cleared of bush all around the outer perimeter by kind permission of a Public Works Department JCB. In the camp, I slept in a small brick building in one corner with the room also doubling as an armoury. The two Wakamba drivers had their own house and the Somalis lived in a long building which I presume must have at one time been a hospital ward.

The first internal operation was launched in the area north of the Tana River (where during Ramadan the riverine tribesmen beat out an hypnotic rhythm on their drums all night) and south-west of Meri. We left camp after dark in several Land Rovers, plus an escort for their return journey. Only the two elders and Mohammed, amongst our party, were aware of our destination although the area generally was closed to all security forces because of an impending operation. Closure had to be strictly adhered to for there was always the danger of being fired on by friendly forces, something that happened too often during the Mau Mau emergency.

I opted for long khaki trousers, a bush shirt and a shabby old scarecrow type hat which mirrored about half the party, whilst the remainder wore chukas. When getting into the vehicle in camp, I spoke to one of the Somalis who failed to identify me through my dark make-up for a good twenty seconds.

On debussing from the vehicles we went to ground in some thick bush that was, we were reliably informed, several miles away from the nearest manyatta, and tucked ourselves away for the night. Each man had a blanket, a canvas *chargul* holding a couple of litres of water, a little rice, tea and sugar plus, of course, his rifle and a plentiful supply of ammunition. I had selected a really snug ·3006 sporting rifle (a Winchester, in fact); I also had a Sterling SMG strapped across my back and a phosphorus grenade in my back pocket to cause a diversion if I had to run for it! Young Mohammed remained in close proximity with a small haversack containing spare ammunition and a few good ·36 grenades. For the one and only time, we carried a radio as I was not sure how the group would react if we came under fire, particularly if we encountered a gang much bigger than ourselves. (We were in the region of twenty men, all of whom were armed.) The radio was also some sort of limited insurance for myself, the only non-Somali in the group. We found at dawn that we had indeed selected a good site and, although we could hear camels bellowing during the day, we were not disturbed. Apart from water nothing else passed our lips all day.

It had been decided that should a herdboy stumble across us, he would be kept at arm's length for fear he should identify me, the only weak link in the group. Should he catch sight of me, then he would be taken into custody and held until the operation was over, when he would be released unharmed.

The plan was for us to layup during the day, moving only at night-time when I would take up a position towards the rear of the patrol. As we lay there taking advantage of what little shade the thorn trees afforded, Mohammed, who was sharing the same bush as me, was watching a giant green and red hopper shedding its old skin and then ambling away in its new finery.

'Why can't we be like that?' whispered the young man; a very philosophical point that helped to relieve the boredom, it being almost too hot to think.

The Somalis were much better at selecting a good shady area. They did it instinctively; whilst I thought I had found a good spot, only to have to move in an hour or so when the sun moved relentlessly on.

Just before dusk we all headed towards the horizon where sounds heard during the day seemed to indicate the presence of a manyatta. We moved away in two groups with the only audible noise being the shuffling of sandals. The first group went ahead, approaching the manyatta that had three small huts. As they got nearer the dogs started to bark and the noise of a wedding feast within grew quieter as the occupants asked who was approaching. My group took up a position on the other side of the manyatta, and sat down in some bushes that fortunately had not been used as a latrine.

Mohammed was translating for me: the group had gone into the manyatta in a high-handed manner that any *Shifta* gang would have been proud of. They were received with some warmth and offered food and drink which they gratefully accepted and, as they were part of a large gang who had just arrived from Somalia, could they have some food for their colleagues outside? A few minutes later one of the Pseudos came out with a *karai* full of delicious camel meat. I had eaten camel before but nothing like this. According to Mohammed, it had been chopped up into small pieces and then fried an oil.

The camel's milk I passed over as I never grew to like its smoky taste and would only drink it if I was desperate. It also had the effect of causing havoc with my bowels!

We left the manyatta to its feast and, telling them that we were heading east, took off to the west, normal *Shifta* craft, and split into two groups hiding our tracks, we hoped, along camel paths until we were well away from the area.

Before dawn we found another larger manyatta where the occupants were still asleep. Whilst the rest of us went to hide ourselves in the bush, two Pseudos remained behind and spoke to the early risers before rejoining us. I was eager to know what my chaps had picked up. It seemed that we were the only gang seen in the area during the past week. Prior to that, two small gangs had passed through and it was thought that they might be heading towards Mbalambala, where there was a trading centre and police post. At the wedding feast there was a game scout from Garissa who said that he was on leave and that at work he normally patrolled with a ·375 rifle. He also said that he was thinking of joining the *Shifta* and that if he did so he would take his rifle with him. His card was duly marked.

The patrol continued for a week, the little food that we needed being provided by the manyattas that we visited, where we also replenished our water. Laying up all day observing the movements of the local population was both boring and at times quite physically tiring. We were plagued by camel flies: large yellow jobs who could survive a hefty blow. In fact the only sure way to render them harmless seemed to be to decapitate them; even then they wandered around for a while, not convinced that they were dead. I made a mental note to try and obtain some green mosquito nets, which would have the dual role of keeping mosquitoes and camel flies at bay in addition to aiding camouflage.

We continued to pick up information on the movements of small gangs of *Shifta*, all of whom seemed to be moving in the direction of Mbalambala, so I thought it worth while to send a radio message back to Garissa. The radio was switched on and, after establishing that there was no movement within our immediate vicinity, I attempted to raise Garissa but to no avail. I did however pick up RAF Eastleigh, some 250 miles away in

Nairobi, and passed the information through a very competent RAF operator.

There were only two other incidents worthy of note that occurred during the remainder of the week. Just before dawn one morning, very shortly after we had finished our nightly amble, we had just got our heads down when a shot rang out. Crawling over to one of the sentries, I asked what had happened. He said that he had seen an armed man and had fired a shot at him. This seemed odd but I made no comment whilst I lay alongside him and scanned the scrub in the direction he had indicated. There was no movement. Eventually the sentry admitted that he had been playing around with his rifle and that he had accidentally fired it! We broke camp immediately and moved a few miles away just in case someone came to investigate. It is a fact of life that whilst the wide open spaces of Africa look empty and free of people, there are always ears and eyes around, particularly when you don't need them.

The following day we watched the movement of stock and people in and out of a manyatta. Although we were some distance away, Mohammed said that one person who had entered could possibly be one of his attackers. In a quiet moment he had told us about his torture at the hands of the *Shifta*. They had in fact pegged him out on the ground saying that as he worked for a 'Nazerine', he would die like one, and they then carried out the 'Crucifixion'. After the *Shifta* had left, sympathetic friends had cut him free and placed him on a bed, where we found him.

It was late afternoon but with plenty of light left when we sent one group of Pseudos into the manyatta whilst the remainder, including Mohammed and myself, went to ground in the scrub on the other side. After some time the peace was shattered by shouts of alarm as a lone figure tore out of the manyatta and headed straight for us. A wild-eyed Somali with a huge mop of black hair, he was carrying a spear and dressed only in a *kikoi* and sandals. In what seemed like a couple of minutes, he was on top of us and a wild scramble developed as we tried to subdue him. The hand-to-hand struggle became very violent during which time our visitor got a glimpse of my face which, although additionally darkened by several days' growth of beard, was undoubtedly that of a white man. His death was welcomed by Mohammed, for he was indeed one of his attackers; but it was really a blow to our plan of capturing a member of a *Shifta* gang to gain intelligence and perhaps even of turning him.

Some of the Pseudos came from the manyatta and told us the full story. When they had entered the manyatta they were welcomed and offered food and drink. As they drank camels' milk their hosts told them that there was another stranger (i.e. *Shifta*) in the manyatta and that he had inquired whether there were any security forces in the area, as he had heard a shot very early that morning! As they made suitable conversation, the 'stranger' suddenly appeared in the doorway of the hut, took one look at the occupants and fled. It seemed certain that he had identified one of our party as a 'wrong 'un' and had fled for his life.

The team did recover a small haversack that he had left behind. This only contained personal items such as a leather amulet containing extracts from the Koran. As no shots had been fired, we decided to carry the body away with us and bury the corpse elsewhere. The site of the struggle was re-arranged, holes were dug and the area used as a latrine, and the inhabitants of the manyatta told that the stranger that had run away had a long-standing blood feud with one of our gang, and that he fled fearing retribution. We buried the *Shifta* several hours later on the site of a deserted manyatta which was full of rubbish.

Next morning we moved to our rendezvous point and a few hours later Dougie Hughes and company arrived to collect us. Sitting next to Dougie on the way back to Garissa, I apologised for my physical state, telling him that the only water that had come my way during the previous week had been to drink. I hoped that my body smell was not too high.

'You stink to high heaven,' he replied and then he smiled and said, 'It's good to see you back,' which for him was quite a speech. A character with a dry sense of humour, Dougie had a personal card engraved 'Cynic and Sonneteer'.

Back in camp we discussed the patrol and what exactly we had a achieved, if anything. It had certainly improved our learning curve of how the *Shifta* operated and how they received a large amount of passive support from the local Somali population. It had also thrown up the difficulty of operating with the inclusion of a white man in the Pseudos, particularly with the lack of natural cover i.e. forest areas that were a boon to Pseudo operations during the Mau Mau emergency. The lack of such cover made moving around during the hours of daylight difficult. My Somalis made it clear that they preferred me to be with them; the possibility of being hit by our own security forces weighed heavily in this decision. Our best bet, the group thought, lay in hit-and-run operations the other side of the border, plus the occasional operation against an identified gang when it was located in the Garissa district.

The RAF had been asked if they could fly one of their Canberra P19 reconnaissance jets in the proximity of the Somali border to photograph any areas that could be presumed to be suspicious, either because of the presence of above-average population or the actual siting of camps surrounded by thorn zaribas. I was told that flights had not revealed anything that the photographic interpreters considered out of the ordinary.

I had asked for a supply of green mosquito nets from the Quartermaster. A consignment of snow-white nets arrived; obviously the QM thought white to be a more worthwhile shade! With the aid of some strong green dye purchased from local trading stores, the nets and our hands were soon dyed a dark green. When lying up in the scrub under the nets, we felt we were really hidden from the *Shifta* and most likely from any wandering Canberras.

A radio link from our base camp enabled us to communicate with both the Police and Army operations rooms. Reg Perkins, a Special Branch technical officer, laid on a field telephone link from my house and armoury to another building that was used by the sentries. Unbeknown to any of the other camp staff, the field telephone masked the bugging of the building in question. If we took any prisoners, they were to be housed in that building; it would then have been possible to monitor their conversations from my house where we also kept the lorry batteries that would power the microphone.

Reg provided us with some amusement when he stepped blind off a ladder into a bucket of whitewash à là Laurel and Hardy. Reg has generous dimensions and I think he found the Frontier heat uncomfortable, and he could not wait to get back to Nairobi. Perhaps it was inside knowledge but whenever I visited Nairobi in the months ahead, it was not unusual to see his Peugeot 404 saloon parked outside an office or hotel. When he left his Trilby on the rear parcel shelf, one knew instinctively that someone was getting the benefit of his technical expertise.

Sometimes of an evening I would be invited to have dinner with Irene and Dougie Hughes, who had a double-storey house in Garissa, a fact that I shall always remember as the roof space harboured a host of bats who stank the place out. These breaks, bats aside, were most welcome. After driving down alone on a couple of occasions I was reminded that there was an emergency on and that in future I should bring an escort! This I did, not wishing to run any unnecessary risks.

In camp, routine training work continued: the two Wakamba askaris, the only non-Somalis I shared the camp with, honing the weapons skills of the Pseudos. The latter were always keen to learn and most became proficient shots. Kit was overhauled and the defensive perimeter wire fence and zariba kept clear of rubbish and repaired where game had infiltrated. One morning a sentry reported finding two pieces of cloth tied to one of the thorn trees that made up the zariba. Closer examination showed traces of blood on the barbed wire. Clearly someone was probing the camp perimeter.

That day I went into Garissa and told Dougie of my plans for that evening, and also took the opportunity to read up intelligence reports from other stations in the North-Eastern Province and the old style NFD, in addition to the overall country-wide intelligence summaries produced weekly by SB HQ. *Shifta* ambushes, killings and abductions continued throughout the province, as the attackers struck when and where they wanted, knowing that the local population would provide them with food and drink in addition to keeping them informed on the movements of the security forces. I spoke to

Baramadei to find out what was being said about the Pseudo camp and called upon the Lieutenant-Colonel commanding the Kenya Army camp.

The Colonel was a Mkamba who had risen through the ranks. He was an affable type, ready to cooperate and well aware of the dangers of our two units unintentionally clashing in the areas this side of the border. Wherever possible we fixed our operational boundaries using tracks, these being more readily recognised by strangers to the area than a dry *lagh* or *donga*. During our friendly chat over coffee in the tented operational room, the Colonel told me that should my camp be attacked, he would send in his armoured cars with their ·5 machine-guns firing. I told him that this was very kind. But could the Army wait until we fired 3 red Verey lights? Otherwise there might be a danger of hitting my men, some of whom could be outside the perimeter defences or otherwise exposed. The Colonel also told me that I could make use of his first-class medical section. This was a most useful meeting which highlighted once again how important periodic liaison meetings are.

Just before dusk that evening, a party of twelve Pseudos moved out of the camp and took up ambush positions in the area where someone had tied parts of a chuka to a thorn tree. Those remaining in the camp were on stand-by with instructions not to fire unless told to do so by a recognisable voice from one of us. It was a very clear night with bright stars in abundance; the lights of Garissa *boma* were clearly visible and anyone moving in our vicinity should be clearly seen. Not knowing from what direction our attackers might come, for we were convinced that this was the work of the *Shifta*, we lay up in a semi-circle, each man about a yard apart. Distant noises from a manyatta apart, the only sounds we heard were that of a prowling jackal and a gerenuk (a long-necked gazelle) that snorted on detecting us and crashed away.

Well after midnight, one of the Pseudos went into convulsions then lapsed into unconsciousness. Going to his aid, I found the man, one of our toughest operators who had performed well on cross-border raids, was as stiff as a board and I feared that he had been bitten by a cobra or mamba. He was taken at some speed to the Kenya Army camp where a very efficient medical orderly diagnosed that the man had been stung by a particularly virulent scorpion. Apparently his skin had one puncture instead of the two a snake would inflict. Whatever medical treatment he was given, the man in question was back on his feet within twenty-four hours, his nervous system having fully recovered from the scorpion sting. The camp was not attacked and there was no more probing of our perimeter defences.

The arrival of an armoured Land Rover (another point raised with the Commissioner during his visit to Garissa) created a stir within the camp and elsewhere. The doors were fitted with steel plates and the windscreen, which was still glass, had restricted vision, almost like a visor since the edges were also reinforced with steel plates. The vehicle was used for a while as a prototype, and one did feel safer when traversing the lonely border tracks. The vehicle was masterminded by Bob Jones, the Force Transport Officer (FTO), and was a good example of local improvisation. The drawback was its weight as the vehicle became quickly bogged down during the rains.

There was an amusing incident at the camp one day when I was absent in Garissa. A GSU Inspector visited the camp to see the famous Land Rover. He picked the wrong vehicle and, before the drivers could stop him, he tested the vehicle's resistance to a ·38 bullet and put a hole in the aluminium door of a standard vehicle. His embarrassment was still evident a few weeks later when he escorted my group to the border and I had to 'swim' his Land Rover across a raging torrent in Lagh Bogal. We landed some way downstream and I was not entirely certain that we would make it but it was just my way of showing my appreciation!

There was another local matter to deal with, and this concerned the pro-*Shifta* activities of our friend the retired Somali Sub-Inspector. Now known to the Pseudos as 'Waraba' (the Hyena or in this context, more correctly the Hermaphrodite Dog!), this individual had stock both sides of the border and also a couple of trading stores within the NFD. There was reliable information that he was supplying the *Shifta* with details of our movements and also identifying individual

members of the Pseudo team. It was a pity that he never visited
our camp. We had a pow-wow with the team elders, the
outcome of which was that a decision was taken to launch a
propaganda campaign against him with the aim of discrediting
him in the eyes of the Somali authorities. An erudite Somali
concocted suitable letters on the NPPPP notepaper that had
been seized earlier. The letters, addressed to government
officials in the Lower Juba Province, pointed out that whereas
the former Sub Inspector openly purported to be assisting the
Greater Somalia cause, he was in fact in league with Kenya
government officials from whom he gained considerable
financial and trading benefits; in fact he was lining his pockets
to the detriment of the cause. The letters were posted in Nairobi
because of local border closures. A couple of months later, the
individual concerned took off for Somalia, as he had heard that
his camels and cattle had been confiscated.

It was time to carry out another cross-border operation. This
time the area chosen, known locally as Darkenli, does not
appear on any map that I have seen. But I believe that it lies in
the vicinity of the Somali village of Fafdo, which is situated
midway between the Kenya border posts of Liboi and Dif. The
large *Shifta* camp (though the Somalis always exaggerated
their reports and rarely if ever spoke of a small camp) was said
to consist of a mixture of *Shifta* and Somali Gendarmerie.

We gathered together, rather than paraded, late one afternoon when weapons and equipment were checked. Each man
carried his own personal rifle and ammunition, a full chargul,
blanket and mosquito net and, in a small haversack, two ·36
grenades and a small packet of rice, plus what other small items
of food he wished to carry. I had my SMG, with my ·3006
strapped across my back. In other respects my equipment
matched that of my Somali colleagues, with the exception that
my ·36 grenades were of the booby-trapped variety. In camp I
slept with the good grenades on one side of the bed and the
dodgy items on the other side. It was true that I did sometimes
have dreams, but never quite nightmares, of mixing the two
items up. But the boxes were kept locked and I had the
only key. As a last ditch check, the person who prepared the
booby-trapped grenades (which would explode once the lever

was released), had coated the detonators with white talcum powder.

On this occasion we left for the border just about at dusk with an escort provided by the Kenya Army; in fact some of the Pseudos had exciting rides sitting on the hatchways of the Ferret scout cars that sped across the firmer parts of the track at about 50 mph. A couple of odd shots were fired at the convoy but we did not stop. One Pseudo, who had been holding on to a whip aerial arrived clutching just a small section left at the base, claiming that the top half had been shot away. But the scout car crew said that the aerial had most likely had a natural fracture.

As we disembarked near the border, I could hear the soldiers passing whispered comments on my rag-bag group and the foolhardy *mzungu* (white man) who accompanied them. The gist of their remarks was that the Pseudos would keep going and not come back.

Moving off with our now familiar shuffling motion with the two elders leading and Mohammed bringing up the rear, with myself in the position immediately ahead of him, the only other sound was the movement of charguls against our bodies, a sort of mild thump. After the relatively open scrub of the border area, we moved into some thicker bush with the ubiquitous *nyika* (an acacia with vicious long thorns) being too many for comfort. We closed ranks as we sought to remain in contact and stopped from time to time to listen and also check for the smell of smoke. At one such stop one of the leaders said he could smell wood smoke and this was soon followed by the sound of dogs barking. Moving cautiously, we could soon hear muffled voices, and bending over double so as not to present an outline against the night sky, we crept slowly forward aware that the dogs were now beginning to get more excited and that it would not be long before somebody challenged us. We had agreed beforehand that if we were detected by dogs, we should launch the attack right away. Each Pseudo would throw one or more grenades, depending on the time element, and fire into the camp before we headed back to the border.

Dust and smoke were everywhere as I fired a long burst into a mass of shadowy figures, some of whom were moving away from the flickering flames of the fire, alarmed by the dogs'

frantic barking and grenades exploding. There were cries of
pain and a lot of shouting as grenades and rifle shots continued
to explode in or over the thorn zariba around the *Shifta* camp. It
was only due to careful pre-planning and discipline amongst
the Pseudos that we withdrew without too much panic and as
one group. There was to be no running and each man was to
check on and stay close to his neighbour.

In fact we headed back for the border at a very smart pace: on
some occasions almost running, particularly when shots winged
overhead and we could hear the angry voices of our pursuers.
It was clear that behind us was a very angry bunch of men: the
target area was alive with noise and shouts from our flanks
indicated that the pursuit was from more than one direction.
After half an hour or so, we slowed our pace and confirmed,
once again, that we were all present. We stopped for a while to
see if there was anyone close on our tail and I took the
opportunity to carelessly drop my haversack that contained
two very dodgy ·36 grenades. We sat down and spread
ourselves around for a couple of minutes so that anyone
following up our tracks the next morning could not fail to miss
the stopping point and would certainly discover the bundle
that had been seeded for them.

There was an audible sigh as we got moving once again and
sheer joy when we reached the welcome cut-line that marked
the Kenya border. But we kept on the move for another couple
of hours before settling down for the night in a thicket of thorn-
trees, hoping that we would not disturb the vicious little red
ants that bit like mad and always seemed to nest there. After a
few hours' rest, but not too much sleep, we moved on again
shortly before dawn as we wanted to put more ground between
us and our pursuers...

As we had water, we avoided the established and well-used
water-holes and kept well away from Lagh Bogal where there
was bound to be a concentration of stock and watchful
herdboys. We moved in two lines roughly parallel to each other
but some twenty yards apart; both as an anti-ambush drill and
also to confuse any would-be trackers, who would find
following the spoor difficult over the gravel surface that we
were now covering. This was exactly the type of terrain where

at the onset of the rains I had witnessed tadpoles swimming in clear pools of rain water, in an area that had not had any rain for many months. In fact we did not see any humans or stock that day and we finally went to ground when the sun was at its peak and the heat casting mirages on the ground.

Most of the Pseudos prayed whenever they could and they would go through the cleansing ritual using some of their drinking water. In fact most of them would finish their water supply before me, and when I queried this they would reply, 'N, Shallah' (God willing). In other words they were in the Lord's hands.

Whether it was night or day, whenever I left the campsite to relieve myself, I was conscious that one of the group would always follow me at a discreet distance. They got to know that I am a very light sleeper, and that often in the night I would go for a prowl round and then settle down on a fresh bit of ground, with a haversack as my pillow and one small blanket, to resume my slumbers. They never questioned my actions.

When it was possible to light a fire, I shared some boiled rice with them adding my own luxury of packet soup. I found that I could go several days on this meagre diet in the NFD, as long as there was water around.

On this particular patrol the intention was to walk back to Garissa, calling in at the occasional manyatta, and generally behaving as a *Shifta* gang would, coming in from Somalia. We sighted a manyatta as dawn was just about on us, and we went to ground and watched the break-of-day activities; camels and goats were being milked, and then led out to graze. When the manyatta was fully abuzz, a small section of Pseudos went into what we could now see was a large encampment. Though some of the huts were of a more permanent variety. Most of the huts were of the type that could be erected or dismantled in a couple of hours. The huts, or *gureis*, consisted of camel 'Herios' saddles or mats that were strung over a framework of curved sticks. It was quite a sight to see Somali (or Boran, for that matter) camel trains on the move with the curved sticks protruding fore and aft of the camels, on top of which were perched pregnant women, the elderly and young goats.

Hiding up in the scrub, we could hear the exchange of

greetings, 'Nabat', as the Pseudos were apparently welcomed and then suddenly there was a commotion and a lone figure fled the manyatta, too far away from any of the two groups for them to take action. A lone, unarmed *Shifta* had got away, probably because he had recognised someone in our group. The consensus was that the man in question was most likely a scout, sent out to gather information or perhaps search for food.

The Somalis in the manyatta were very suspicious of my group and sullenly refused to talk about the stranger who had fled. After a quick search of the huts, the place where the stranger had been sleeping was identified and, after a consultation with the elders amongst the Pseudos, it was decided that the hut be emptied of all goods and then burnt. This was done by Somali on Somali, with myself on this occasion an interested onlooker in the bush appreciating the value of indigenous justice. No one was harmed and under the emergency regulations the need for instant punishment had been met.

We moved on quickly, splitting up and rejoining again to present a confused pattern of tracks to any would-be followers. During the late afternoon, we came in sight of a small 'pan' (water-hole) that was surrounded by small thorn trees. The absence of any stock tracks seemed to indicate that the pan was not being used by local tribesmen, possibly because of the lack of nearby grazing. But even so we made a cautious approach until the pan, and the large bull elephant that was right in the middle, was in clear view.

The bull detected us and he flapped his ears and trumpeted his displeasure. He was not keen to give ground and he made several mock charges before he loped away, clearly upset at being shifted. We had not won much of a victory. The water was only a few inches deep, dark green in colour and also very slimy. Pretending not to notice the rank odour, we happily washed our hands and faces and then drank greedily. Some of the more adventurous actually bathed in the murky waters whilst I moved away to be sick, the green slime turning my stomach over.

After moving a safe distance away, we settled down for the night knowing that the following day we would be within walking distance of our camp. A fire was lit, very smoky as we only had the green thorn bush for fuel; and some rice, and a couple of chickens that had been liberated from the manyatta, were cooked.

The devout prayed and after prayers they sat around chatting away in a much more light-hearted way now that the pressures of the patrol were nearly at an end. Apart from the two sentries, the remainder sat around the fire talking about things that were dear to them. The topics were stock (particularly camels and cattle) and their wives and lovers. They were inquisitive about *Ferenjis* (Europeans) and they questioned me about wives: how many can one have and whether families lived together in groups? The bulk of the area that made up the NFD was a single posting for government officers, particularly for Europeans, and the Somalis thought that my wife was waiting for me in Nairobi. They could not understand, how a man of thirty-three had no wife or children. 'Who looks after your stock?'

In turn they told me about their customs and traditions. The Somalis practise female circumcision after which the woman is sewn up, leaving only a small gap for the normal functions. They said that the infibulation presents the groom with a difficult job on his wedding night, as failure will invite scorn from his bride!

Nobody slept much that night and many throats were husky next morning as tales were told well into the small hours.

Although deep down my Somalis saw themselves as different to the African, they had a realistic streak in them which told them that their new masters would not interfere with their nomadic way of life, religion and customs.

After a quick slop in the slime to rid myself of the last remaining traces of brown make-up, we set off just before dawn as we wanted to reach camp during the hours of daylight. The nearer we got to base the more tense we became, as we knew that this was the most dangerous time for us as we moved into an area where security force patrols, both in vehicles and on foot, were more active. I moved to the front of the patrol and removed my headgear, hoping that beneath the grime and whiskers it was possible to identify a *mzungu*.

At a crossroad of some dusty tracks we were astonished to

find a deserted trader's store in pristine condition. The thatch roof was undisturbed and the wooden framework free of bullet holes, and no attempt had been made to burn the structure down. Having seen the skeletal remnants of stores that had been ransacked, burnt and plundered in various locations (including Jara Jila, Bura and numerous other sites) the sight of this charmed building seemed miraculous, until one of our knowledgeable local experts explained that the store was owned by our friend the Sub-Inspector ... Well, that explained it. We gathered round the store, our admiration turning to anger as the true significance of the store's survival sank in. What should we do?

'Choma,' (burn) said the Pseudos. I agreed with them and put the phosphorus grenade in the thatch myself, pausing only briefly to make sure the job was done properly, before moving away quickly once again back into the scrub that gave us a modicum of cover.

We arrived back in camp well before dusk, and I went ahead alone for the last few hundred yards to lessen the risk of an armed confrontation.

As usual, we held a post-*baraza* (meeting) to chew over our successes and failures. There was general consensus that internal operations were very risky and for the effort put into them not very productive. The risks were largely the fear of being attacked by our own security forces, although the fear of betrayal by the local population also figured prominently. I did try a few patrols combining my Pseudos with a GSU patrol commanded by John Atkinson, the officer commanding E Company, with whom I had worked closely prior to my forming the Somali Pseudos. He was reliable and effective. In fact I had given him the nickname of 'Boots', such was his persuasive powers in getting curfew breakers to open their doors after they had been caught out in the open and fled to the sanctity of a hut.

We did several joint patrols around the Garissa area, usually acting on information but none were successful. There was a natural suspicion between his askaris and my Pseudos although they did operate together: one occasion we were not far off a contact, which fell through when the game scout who was leading us to a *Shifta* gang got cold feet at the last moment, leading us away from the gang as he feared for his family, who were Somali.

On the second patrol, we accompanied a couple of platoons of the newly formed Kenya Army Parachute Section. The soldiers were smartly dressed in jungle greens and green scarfs which looked really sartorial and perhaps a trifle overdressed for an NFD patrol. The section was commanded by Simon Combes, a former King's African Rifles officer, whom I had not previously met. In later years Simon made a name for himself as an artist who specialised in wildlife subjects.

We stayed out on patrol together for several days, sleeping in the open with the usual blanket but being more daring, having a fire to cook on every night and more in the way of sentries on guard.

The two groups tolerated each other and we did try to work together, although the undercurrent of mistrust was never far away. The soldiers told my Pseudos that they thought the unit too small to be patrolling for *Shifta* in the remoteness of the NFD. In fact we must have totalled some 40 armed men. My men were frightened that if we did contact a gang, they might be shot in the ensuing fire fight. What passed from my men to the Pseudos I have no idea, but I doubt that they said very much. Relations between Simon, who had the task of training the embryo parachute unit, and myself were good. Apart from gathering some low-grade intelligence on *Shifta*, we achieved very little. It is not wise, I came to learn, to combine Pseudo irregulars with established security force personnel on operations, and we stopped such combined operations. The idea of the Pseudos gathering good intelligence and then bringing the superior firepower of the Army or GSU in to hit the *Shifta* was tempting but it never came to fruition.

Time was drawing near for me to go on leave to the UK and I had made it known both to Dougie Hughes and David Wadely, a former Assistant Commissioner of Police, Special Branch, and now Security Advisor to Special Branch, that on return from leave I wanted to do something else in SB and not return to the NFD.

What had the Pseudo operations achieved? At that time we were the only such outfit operating in the NFD, although a little later on Peter England was sent to Mandera to start a similar outfit – a task he disliked immensely for he was a city gent who had no particular attachment to the wilds. I shared a house with Peter and several others in Nairobi at one time and it came as a big shock when, several years later, I heard of his suicide, brought on by being blackmailed by some Somalis whom he had met whilst in Mandera. Peter was an upright citizen who should have cried for help; instead he chose to take what he believed was the honourable way out.

There is no doubt that the Pseudo operations had worried the *Shifta*. We were a very small body whose overheads were modest. We had taken the fight to the gangs on their home ground, inflicted casualties and caused some confusion amongst both gangs and their passive supporters (so that they did not know whom to trust). Even then reports were coming in about armed *Shifta* incursions into Kenya, in the Ijara area, where, in two separate attacks, two *Shifta* were killed by the premature explosions of the grenades that they had just hurled. *Shifta* gangs were usually composed of more men than they had firearms for. When someone was killed or badly wounded, one of the spearmen would take up his weapon whilst others would attempt to remove the body.

On one occasion we stopped an ox that was crossing the border into Somalia, with a badly wounded *Shifta* lying strapped to its back and covered by a blanket. The Somalis driving the beast said that the man had been knifed in a brawl. But it was clear that the wounds were from bullets and the sub-section of the Herti tribe to which they belonged was heavily involved with the *Shifta*. There was also the fact that medical attention in Garissa would have been more easily accessible. For the record, the ox and its cargo were allowed to proceed as it was doubtful whether the wounded man would last much longer. We ourselves did not have a radio and if any of our party had been wounded then the journey back to medical treatment would have been equally torturous.

The morning finally came to say 'Nabad gelyo' (Goodbye) to the group, as I left camp for the last time. I gave Mohammed some *dia* (blood money) as he had been badly injured in my employ. The group would remain in the camp with the two Wakamba askaris until a new officer arrived to take over. I left with mixed feelings as there was sadness at leaving a loyal bunch of Somalis. I had not had any defections although a few weeks later one man did defect to Somalia with his rifle. But in the main I was pleased to be going as I felt that I had had enough of Pseudo operations and, as an expatriate in an independent Kenya, perhaps it was time for a local officer to take over and show his mettle.

There is one footnote to add. For some time various officers, myself included, had been lobbying Police Headquarters in an effort to get Baramadei promoted to Inspector. The rules at that time were that African candidates for promotion to Inspector had to be fully literate. Unfortunately, Baramadei, who spoke Somali, Boran, English and some Italian, was not fully literate in English as his written knowledge of the language was poor. Even as I left, the battle continued and I hope that the promotion was eventually granted as he was a good officer and really deserved upgrading. In the years that have passed since I left Kenya, I have tried on several visits to make contact again with him but without success.

TWO

THE EARLY DAYS:
HOW IT ALL BEGAN

As a young boy I was always deeply attracted to 'real life' adventure, the likes of Benbow, Rodney and Drake, coupled with such splendid tales as *Treasure Island* and *Robinson Crusoe*. It was particularly the sea that took my early fancy and I believe that a few hundred years back I could readily have been a buccaneer of a more acceptable kind, such as Drake who plundered widely but usually did so in the name of his Queen and Country.

It was not too much of a shock to my parents when I asked to go to sea school. This I did at the age of fourteen when I joined the School of Engineering and Navigation in Poplar, East London. Entry was by way of a personal interview plus the usual written testimony from my secondary school. My parents lived in Bromley, Kent and I had a daily bus trip to and from Poplar, using the old Blackwell tunnel that was originally constructed in the days of horse-drawn vehicles. In those days the East India docks were full of ships and the funnels of various shipping companies could be seen on virtually every horizon. There was the magic of the ship's chandlers, stores full of exciting commodities that, with the possible exception of an African trading store, has no modern counterpart.

We had some good teachers at the school; and I can recall with nostalgia two of the most popular. The first was Captain Willis who, if my memory serves me, had an Extra Master's Certificate in Steam and a Master's Certificate in Sail. In the mid

1940s, Captain Willis must have been approaching sixty. He was a genial and kindly man with a mischievous smile and he kept us deeply involved in our lessons by interspersing the content with 'real life' tales from the Seven Seas. Captain Willis took us for the whole range of nautical subjects, ranging from Oceanography, Seamanship and Morse to Rules of the Road and Knot Tying. One day, when we had a rare outing manning a whaler down at the East India Docks, the Captain gave us the order with a wicked grin, 'When I say grab the oars, I don't mean grab the whores.'

Such innocent little asides endeared him to the budding cadets.

We also continued with our lay studies and it is here that my second recollection comes in. Our Maths teacher was known as 'Pip'. A smart man who wore good quality tweed suits and bow ties, he had a cutting wit and a good rapport with the pupils. At that time I was good at Maths; later when we moved on to Astro-navigation I declined in status. Anyway, Pip had set us a couple of problems and I was one of the few to get both right. To my detriment I had decided to give an alternative answer to the second question which concerned one of those 'running taps, filling a bath' questions that is loved by examiners. My second answer pointed out that because of the overflow, the bath was unlikely ever to fill up! To my embarrassment he read the second answer out in front of the whole class and then added, 'Franklin, one of your ancestors vanished in mysterious but glorious circumstances in trying to discover the North-West passage. You, my boy, I fear, will simply vanish.' What a character.

The majority of pupils studying Navigation went into the Merchant Navy, but I think fewer of the Engineering students did so.

I left Sea School in 1947 and shortly after my 16th birthday I set off on the Anglo Saxon tanker (the transportation side of Shell) *Nicania*, bound from Thames Haven to Buenos Aires. I was an apprentice on a four year indenture and the world was mine.

My apprenticeship indenture was for four years with a total salary of £390, made up of £75 in the first year, £90 in the

second, £105 in the third and £120 in the final year. The
document also stated that I would be supplied with all 'meat
and drink and lodging' but that I had to supply my own
clothing. At one time apprentices had to supply their own
bedding but this sub-para was erased from my indenture. My
uniform and working apparel cost my parents well over £100, a
difficult sum for them to find in those post-war times and I
know that my father, a strong trade unionist and labour
supporter, received assistance from Albert V. Alexander, First
Lord of the Admiralty in Churchill's wartime government. A.
V. Alexander had considerable experience of Merchant Navy
affairs and he found some fund that paid towards my parents'
expenditure.

Life for a young cadet was exciting and the combination of
fresh air (very fresh in winter in the North Atlantic) and
foreign ports was this schoolboy's dream. As cadets we
lived and dined amongst the officers although the bulk of
our working days was spent with the seamen. There were
limited occasions when we were allowed on the bridge for
navigation lessons, but of course we did take our turn at the
helm and as lookout on the foredeck. I suppose that as
cadets we were neither officers nor seamen and that we had
to run the gauntlet of trying not to offend either side. When
the ordinary seaman refused to clean out the cargo tanks
with caustic soda, by hand, claiming that the levels of toxic
fumes from the last cargo were too high, the cadets joined
the able seamen in doing the job because it had to be done.
The fact that we got a little heady from the gas and suffered
mild burns from the caustic soda was, we thought, all part
of the job. As cadets we paid £1 a year for membership of
the Navigators' and Engineers' Union but we never saw an
union official and we were totally ignorant of any union
rules.

Tankers in those days still bore some resemblance to ships
and the age of the supertanker was still a few years away. With
a gross tonnage of between eight and ten thousand tons, they
were almost submerged when fully laden and in rough seas it
was sometimes extremely dangerous to walk along the flying
bridge from one end of the ship to the other. On the *Nicania*

there was an inclinometer on the bulkhead outside the cadets' cabin, and it was not uncommon to see it register a 40° roll in a storm.

There was other excitement to contend with on board ship and that was my first encounter with a homosexual. We were warned by the officers to be careful and it therefore did not come as a great surprise to find myself propositioned by the storeman. He was in his fifties, truly an old salt, who possessed all the sailorly skills of canvas sewing, knot and splice making and chasing young cadets when at sea, and when ashore he was amongst the ladies with equal enthusiasm. His nickname was Jumper, as his skin would twitch visibly if someone touched his arm. The trick was to try not to be left alone with him. This was sometimes difficult when you were despatched to fetch a can of paint or fish oil from the dark confines of his store, although one became adept at moving in pairs or at talking to a non-existent person when alone or, if all else failed, in sheer desperation turning on him with a fid or marlinspike. We remained friends, of a distant kind, in spite of his continued enthusiasm.

In 1949 we sailed with a Chinese crew from Rotterdam bound for the Far East. The *Bolma*, only 3,744 gross tons, suffered engine trouble in the Gulf of Suez, the white metal in the bearings having melted, a fact that I remember but cannot claim to fully understand. We were anchored for a week or so whilst experts arrived and repairs carried out.

During one period of inactivity I spied another Shell tanker at anchor loading supplies, and I knew that one of the cadets on board was a buddy from my sea school days in Poplar. So I paid an Egyptian fisherman to ferry me across the bay and called in on my colleague who, strangely enough, was half-Egyptian. Shortly afterwards the *Bolma* pulled up anchor and set sail, leaving me in a great panic at having deserted, or at least left my ship without permission! All ended well. An hour or so later the *Bolma* returned, having completed her engine trials and I went back to her atop a load of fish and nets, and was able to get back up the Jacob's ladder with no one, except my fellow cadets, ever having being aware of my absence!

On the *Bolma* we sailed up the Mekong Delta carrying a cargo of high-octane fuel for the French Air Force. We had an escort of French frigates and a Foreign Legion section on each of the dozen or so vessels in the convoy. Carrying such a volatile cargo, all smoking on board was prohibited except in a very small smoking-room that also served as a reading room. I was horrified to see a Legionnaire smoking on deck as he lay alongside his Bren (which had a curved magazine as opposed to the straight magazine of the Mas 7·5 mm) which was aimed at the river bank through a hawser pipe. The Legionnaire thought at first that I wanted to examine his Bren gun but he did eventually stub his cigarette out.

The next morning, having lost one ship that ran aground after being mined, we commenced discharging our cargo at a Caltex installation that as usual was miles away from any signs of civilisation. We had heard shots in the night from prowling Vietminh and we were advised not to go ashore unless under escort. The Legionnaires, who were also to escort us on the return journey, had transport and were going into the nearest village for supplies ... Would we like to go?

With another cadet, we squeezed into the front cab of an army lorry and off we went. As we approached a dirt crossroad, I heard the Legionnaires shouting excitedly and pointing at an ox-cart that was halted at the junction. The driver put his foot down and the lorry accelerated and caught the obstruction midway between ox and cart. There was an almighty bang, dust and much shouting. The Legionnaires set about the driver of the ox-cart who ran off leaving his poor old ox lying in the ditch. The Frenchmen, it would seem, had thought the set-up was an ambush and they were merely carrying out some defensive driving. We got back to the ship that evening with a good story to tell but I think the Captain (Macnab) was more than concerned about his teenage cadets and all further trips ashore were cancelled.

I ended my apprenticeship with eighteen months of voyaging around the East Indies before paying off at Tilbury in April 1951, having decided that the Merchant Navy was not the life for me. But I had enjoyed my four years and the travel and adventure would stay with me, as would the ability to stand on my own two feet and think for myself.

There are memories of the sea that will remain with me for ever more: the exuberance with which numerous schools of dolphins homed in on a ship and then played host to the vessel like a long-lost friend by swimming on the curve of the bow wave, usually in such close proximity that it was possible to see the button-like aperture on their heads opening and closing as they breathed; nights in the tropics when the whole surface of the sea seemed to be alight, such was the spread of the tiny organisms that make up the wonder of phosphorescence; steering a ship of 10,000 tons through the Suez Canal as a teenager when, due to the very slow speed, it was necessary to move the helm half a turn to port then half a turn to starboard to achieve a satisfactory track and on one occasion, before my seventeenth birthday, a Dutch pilot of the Canal Authority saying to me, 'It's just like driving a car down a narrow road'! (Little did he know that it was to be another five years before I got to drive a car.) There was also the companionship of my fellow cadets, particularly Willy Brown, a short, stocky lad from Birtley in County Durham and Jack Williams, a worldly-wise Scouse from Liverpool.

We had a grizzled old bosun who was more gnome than man. In the summer when he worked stripped to the waist, his skin was like leather. He used to amuse us, when not driving us to work harder, by singing his favourite song, 'Mr Booze'. He also had some helpful advice for young cadets going ashore in foreign parts and I can still hear his rusty voice, as we went down the gangplank in Buenos Aires, croaking out, 'If you're looking for a woman, don't forget to pick an ugly one!'

There were also less amusing incidents: working at the masthead in a heavy swell when, in spite of being well secured, you were conscious that when the ship rolled, you had the sea beneath you not the ship; fighting a fire below deck on an oil tanker dressed in a clumsy asbestos suit and at the end of a life-giving umbilical cord that supplied the oxygen, not being able to see because of the thick smoke, crawling to the base of the fire with the bosun, who was similarly dressed, only to find that we each thought the other had the large foam fire extinguisher;

searching the Chinese crew's quarters for opium before entering port, always a fruitless task made more unpleasant by the
strong smells and the prospect of finding something really foul
lodged in a corner.

My National Service saw me back in the Korean theatre. I had
been in Inchon with the Merchant Navy months before the
outbreak of the North Korean invasion and although I spent
most of my two years in Japan, which I enjoyed immensely, I
did manage two trips to Pusan.

Serving with the 1st Commonwealth Division was an
interesting and I guess an historical occasion, and there was a
wealth of contact with Australian, Canadian and troops from
other Commonwealth and European countries. The majority of
course were Americans and on a couple of occasions we had
misunderstandings despite our common language. The first
took place on a train to Tokyo where we were heading for the
famous 'R and R' leave. An American military policeman
(known as Snowdrops, as they wore white steel helmets)
confiscated my bottle of ginger beer, purchased from the
Australian equivalent of the NAAFI, the Canteen Services, as
alcohol was prohibited on the train! The 'Snowdrops', who
were both black and wearing large ·45 revolvers, would not
believe that ginger beer was a soft drink and the bottle was
thrown out of the window of the Tokyo Express.

The other incident was more amusing. In Tokyo our party
got into conversation with some American soldiers who
thought for some reason beyond me that we were Belgians.
One even asked me, having heard me talking to my colleagues,
whether we spoke English back home in Belgium? Anyway, we
sat together and had a beer whilst we discussed our respective
units. On being asked details of our outfit, I innocently told
them that it was highly unlikely that they would ever have
heard of or come into contact with us, as we operated some way
from the front...

'Hell! You're Commandos,' he said and the next moment we
were then centre of attraction and plied with beer. We did
manage to sneak away eventually, keeping very close to our
chests that we were in fact members of 31 Command Pay

Office, a unit operated by the Royal Army Pay Corps, and camped some distance behind our own lines.

In company with the Black Watch, we sailed home (via Mombasa, where some of the Black Watch disembarked) on the *Empire Fowey*, the same ship that had taken us to the Far East, in July 1953. In a hammock bunk not far away was Cpl. Speakman, VC, and there was some interesting interplay between the Black Watch and the Gordon Highlanders when we arrived at Singapore as the two bands, the Gordons being stationed there, countermarched up and down the quayside in Keppel Harbour, well stoked up with alcoholic refreshment.

My six years floating around the globe did not auger well for a nine-to-five career, and my parents cannot have been too surprised when I informed them, in late 1953, that my application to join the Kenya Police had been successful. I had no police experience and my only knowledge of Kenya was based on the three days we had spent in Mombasa discharging the Black Watch.

THREE

THE WHITE HIGHLANDS

By Christmas I had joined a bunch of hopefuls at a police training camp at Gilgil ('the dusty place'!) in the Kenya Rift Valley. Here in a very basic camp – stone huts with wooden shutters and devoid of any glass, communal latrines and plenty of fresh air – we got down to our initial training which, it was hoped, would enable us to understand the local law, speak some basic Kiswahili, revise the use of small arms and generally to get acquainted with the local ways of the indigenous population. It was a pity that apart from an African servant whom one hired to do the *dhobi* and ironing (and how to use a charcoal iron without letting the cinders fly out and burn your uniform was a must!) we did not come into contact with any other Africans on the training course.

Early in 1954 I was posted to Nanyuki, a small town at the foot of Mount Kenya, that sits astride the Equator, and which was also the centre for a buzzing community of European farmers. Although on the training course a KPR officer had mistakenly posted me to Nairobi, incorrectly assessing me as a city gent. I had in fact swapped postings with Ian Fox, who after a short time in the Police went on to better things with Minets in the insurance world.

Nanyuki was in the White Highlands, an area where only whites were allowed to own land. I was posted, by ASP Alan Layton, right away to command a small post on the farm of W. K. Bastard, known as 'Bwana Bura' by his farm labourers as he always called their work 'Bure' (the Swahili for 'useless'). With me was Ralph Ferrari, a Seychellois, although a few months later he was replaced by Ron Tanner, a red-headed Irishman who amongst many other things was very knowledgeable about motor vehicles.

The farms in the post area were all large, and one Ol Pejeta, a huge ranching estate of about 80,000 acres then, was large enough to get lost on. There were, of course, a considerable number of Africans present, usually set up in small villages or compounds in close proximity to the farmer's house. They would be employed on the farm and in return receive a wage, housing for them and their families, an allocation of some basic food items, including *posho* (ground cornflour, also known in Afrikaans as mealie meal) and skimmed milk from the farmer's own herd. Whilst not overpaid, they were able to own their own sheep and goats, and land was set aside for them to graze on. In my district I had a mixed bag: ranging from Turkana, Samburu and Masai, who were usually employed with stock; Kikuyu who were the artisans, fencers, tractor drivers and *neoparas* (headmen or foremen); and a tribe of aboriginal-type trackers and honey collectors, the N'dorobo.

Police duties were almost wholly concerned with the emergency, the majority of our time taken up with either measures to prevent Mau Mau attacks and stock thefts or, more commonly, investigations after incidents had occurred. Most of the incidents were either stock theft or the theft of other items; but we did have a few murders, usually of Africans (who suffered more than anyone else during the Mau Mau emergency) including the slaughter of some Turkana on the farm of W. K. Bastard, shortly after my arrival in early 1954.

Unlike the forests of Mount Kenya and the Aberdares, the farm lands of Nanyuki were not heavily populated with big game, although elephants passed through on their yearly migrations and the odd bad-tempered rhino would visit. The Uaso Nyiro did have its resident hippo and buffalo herds. Patrols on foot were mounted from the post (named 'Bernings' after a former farm manager, whose house I lived in) covering both isolated river and ravine areas, and by vehicle to the end of the Post district, where the patrol would de-bus, and then patrol on foot back to base. Being in a 'settled' area, it was necessary to challenge before any effort was made to open fire.

The Kiswahili word used was 'Simama' (Halt). The challenge was only given when the situation looked very suspicious and the word was not tossed around lightly.

The first time I shouted out 'Simama' was during a combined operation mounted with other units under the command of Boyce Roberts, a District Officer from the administration. As we were approaching W. K. Bastard's labourers' village late one afternoon, a lone figure leapt over the fence and fled into the bush! Probably an unarmed Mau Mau scout of some kind, he got clean away as I sprayed the surrounding bush with my Second World War Sten gun.

Night ambushes on the Uaso Nyiro saw us charged by both hippo and buffalo, and it was frequently the game animals, and other things that stir in the night, that led to the most excitement.

It is a matter of record that I got my first confirmed kills against the Mau Mau on, or rather in, the Uaso Nyiro River. We had motored out before dawn one morning, and the patrol dropped us at the limit of our boundary that bordered Ngobit Post. As we assembled in the early morning light, at the junction of Ol Pejeta and Ansteys Farm, it was still quite chilly and a slight mist hung over the river banks. For a change we opted to patrol the eastern bank of the Uaso, which was strictly speaking the area of Burguret Post; but I doubted whether they would be this far downriver, so off we went.

It was about midday when I saw some dreadlocks bobbing up and down in front of us as a gang we had flushed took off running in a crouched position. After uttering the magic word 'Simama', we fired a few bursts and pursued them. We quickly arrived at the Uaso, into which they had all leapt, to find a lot of disturbance in the water but nothing else. The river was deep and there were hippo around as well as plenty of large monitor lizards. The latter looked like small crocodiles and make similar splashes as they dive in from the banks; but in reality they are harmless and when cornered they would hiss and that's about all. Nevertheless, I was not keen to join them in the water – until we heard some subdued splashing near a small clump of reeds in the middle of a large pool.

Not wishing to send one of my men where I feared to go, I took the plunge, lowered myself in the water and, keeping my Sterling MGC over my head, I waded on tiptoe, sometimes nearly submerging, until I reached the middle of the pool. Almost at once I could see a hat, of the type worn by farmhands, floating in the weeds. I went to retrieve it and, as I reached out to grab it, the hat moved and a large Kikuyu, with bloodshot eyes and yellow teeth, came at me with a *panga*. He had, it would seem, been totally submerged with the exception of his nose and mouth under the hat, where he could breath. The shock nearly upset my balance and I went backwards, both to escape the panga and also to get my gun to bear. I must have moved instinctively, for I cannot recall pulling the trigger, but water was splashing all over the place, mixed with the smell of cordite and the hope that I had not shot myself in the leg or worse. It was over in twenty seconds and two dead Mau Mau, both armed with home-made guns and carrying knives, left the sanctuary of the weeds and started to float downstream with the current, until the bodies were recovered by the rest of the patrol. Thankfully, my men had not opened fire, as I was so close to the two terrorists that it would have been very difficult to see who was who.

We got the bodies into Nanyuki that same evening, when I had my first meeting with our Special Branch Officer, Peter Laycock, who was shot in the hand by Mau Mau in an operation against the Mohammed Mwai gang.

It was along the banks of the same river, but further East, that we had an interesting patrol one day in the vicinity of Minns' farm. We came across two young lynx (caracal) kittens. The African lynx is a delightful creature, very beautiful to look at and very fierce. Their eyes had just about opened, but they were starving and we thought their mother had been shot or trapped. We took the two kittens back to our post, spitting and snarling. Inspector Ron Tanner and myself got permission from Rodney Elliot, the local game warden who, at that time was stationed at Gatheru on Mount Kenya, to keep the creatures providing that we did not sell them. If one wanted to sell them then first it would have been necessary to buy a trapper's licence.

We also sought advice from Raymond Hook, a farmer and experienced hunter who farmed on Mount Kenya and who was famous, amongst other things, for his herd of zebroids – a cross between a zebra and a horse. Raymond taught us to feed the lynx not only meat but also fur and feather, otherwise the creatures would develop rickets! The lynx were fed a diet of African hares that had been run over rather like the rabbit in the UK, the African hare is about the same size, but live above ground. There was also a plentiful supply of African doves, supplemented with portions from gamebirds.

The lynx grew to some 25 pounds in weight and remained very tame, very tame, that is, for creatures from the wild. Mine used to sleep on the bottom of my bed, leaving for its nocturnal prowls by running up the stone wall and squeezing through the gap between the '*Mbati*' (galvanised roof) and the wall. The lynx would return by the same route in the early hours of the morning, dropping on me with a thump. It was these nocturnal pursuits that began to raise problems for 'Burrp', a name I fashioned, being the closest I could get to the melodic purr the cats made. (They could also produce the most astonishing whistles.) It seemed that the lynx could not resist taking chickens from the 'farm labourers' camps; sooner or later they would be killed. Ron Tanner, who had in the mean time been posted to Gatheru, actually had his lynx killed there for much the same crime.

After about a year, I decided to try and return Burrp to the wild. I had been offered £30 for the animal by a Barclays Bank official in Nairobi but I thought the lynx belonged in the wild. I let him go several miles from the post but he returned to the post a day or so later, thumping down on my bed in the night. I tried once again a few days later, he returned and fussed around me purring wildly. After several more unsuccessful attempts, I took him further afield and this time he did not return. I must admit that as he had not put in an appearance for over a week, I went looking for him. I made his loud purring noise and was rewarded by him looking at me from the shelter of a bush, before he snarled and stalked off. He was a beautiful creature whom I really missed for some time. I still have the photographs of him charging and attacking my small dog: the two would roll over in mock combat, then clean each other before the next bout.

The post Land Rover used to come in for some heavy use and sometimes, with the commitment to constant operational activities, the vehicle was not always serviced on time. My short wheelbase Land Rover, OHMS 5479, had undergone some harsh treatment which had resulted in all the brakes packing up; simply nothing would work. The only means of stopping, once the gears had been fully utilised, was for some askaris to dismount and lean against the vehicle's direction of motion, when, after a few staggered steps, the vehicle usually stopped. By this means the Land Rover was eventually driven into Nanyuki and delivered into the safe hands of Gerry Sollit, the Police District Transport Officer (DTO), whose workshops lay immediately to the rear of the police station.

After we had explained in some detail the only way we knew how to stop the vehicle, Gerry smiled and said he would have a go. He climbed in and headed for his workshop, which was constructed of the infamous mbati, at about 10 mph; changed down into first, tried the brakes and, when this failed, showed his undoubted skill by trying to stop the vehicle by slapping the gear into reverse. Unfortunately, the gearbox was having none of this, and there was a mixture of disbelief and horror on his face, as he hit and badly dented the wall of his workshop!

The emergency was not without its moments of light relief. I had a KPR officer posted to me for a few weeks. He was Italian with very little English or Kiswahili. His stay was brief, as the Immigration Department discovered that he was an illegal immigrant. His name was something like 'Bitsicherri' and he had arrived at Mombasa by ship, where he should have remained until his application for a visa had been processed. Instead, he caught a train to Nanyuki, joined the KPR and was enjoying himself. One morning he shouted loudly, 'Ship, ship'. Not wishing to miss such a sight, as after all we were on the Equator, even though several hundred miles from the sea, I hastened outside to see a large sheep, known as 'rations on the hoof', entangled in the barbed wire running around the post.

The poor Italian was repatriated to Mombasa under escort shortly afterwards. I often wonder what he thought of his brief Kenyan odyssey!

I was only once ever inspected by a Headquarter officer whilst at a police post. George Haddingham, an Assistant Commissioner, with the nickname of 'Gorgeous George' because of his smart turn-out, pounced on us one day. Unhappily the post driver was on leave, my knowledge of vehicles very limited, and in addition I did not have a driving licence! The inspecting officer had the bonnet of the Land Rover opened, peered inside, saw it was just about clean, opened the battery and with a cry of glee announced that there was no water in the thing: the battery was dry! I was then lectured on vehicle maintenance, and quite rightly too; but what was bothering, me was the fact that the vehicle engine was warm since I had been driving the thing half an hour before. It passed unnoticed.

The next drama centred round a room that was used as my bathroom and, when not so occupied, as a cell for prisoners until we could get them into Nanyuki. The inspecting officer wanted to know what the knot-hole in the door was for.

'To keep an eye on the prisoners, sir.'

'What about the askaris ogling you when you have a bath?'

There was no answer to that, so I kept quiet.

Roaming the vast areas of Ol Pejeta, I soon became friendly with the manager John Kenyon and his assistant Phil Lake. I was the latter's best man when he married Vera, a nurse from Nanyuki Cottage Hospital. Vera was given away by Aubrey Aggett, another farmer and neighbour. All the local farmers were very helpful to the police and they always made us welcome, either at special invitations, or when just passing through. It was tragic to read much later that Aubrey's son Neil, who was just a toddler in Kenya, was one of those who died in the custody of the South African Police, whilst helping to develop local trade unions. I felt very strongly for both Aubrey and his wife Joy, for they had been good friends to me in Kenya.

Lady Victoria Fletcher, known as 'Taffy', who farmed in the Ngobit area just outside of my district, was another lovely person. Whenever I was passing she would ask me in for a meal; and even if she was on her way in to town, she would tell the cook to prepare me a meal, and then leave me alone in her home. I met her briefly in the Manor Hotel, Mombasa, whilst on holiday there in 1978, as she was leaving the country. I marched up to her and told her what a good friend she had been to the Kenya Police and she was delighted.

It was Phil Lake who taught me how to traverse the huge paddocks on Ol Pejeta without needing to make lengthy detours to find a gate. Two or three men simply held the wire and the fence runners down, and over the Land Rover sailed. In time Phil and Vera built a new home at Loidian, at the southern end of the estate, bordering Anstey's farm. This made a convenient place to stop when on patrol, and we did so on many occasions.

And it was Percy De Bastard who gave me the nickname of 'Yellowneck', a play on the similarity of my surname with that of the partridge (Francolin) known locally as the yellowneck (*kwale*), a point that both Percy and Aubrey Aggett were keen to emphasise, as they feared that I might take it the wrong way! Percy was a kindly man who lived a little closer to the earth than his relatives. His kitchen was always full of *watoto* awaiting their slice of bread and, even when dining with him, the watoto would come into the kitchen, where we were eating, to get their supper. I believe that Percy later died in Nanyuki as the result of injuries sustained during an attack on him in his home.

As unemployment was high and pay relatively low, most expatriates, even impoverished police officers, employed at least one servant. At Bernings, I had a Mkamba cook who worked wonders with a 'yellowneck' (Francolin partridge) and also kept my uniforms and general dhobi in good condition. There was also the hard work of chopping kuni (firewood) to heat the drums of water and one day, as the result of several entreaties from the cook, who was known as 'Johndo', it was decided to hire a young Turkana lad to do the chopping and any other physical work that the cook found difficult.

Eko, a strapping figure in his late teens, lived in the local Turkana encampment that was sited a few hundred yards from the post, so accommodation problems did not arise. He had the traditional hole drilled just under his lower lip, into which was inserted an ivory plug for adornment. Without the plug in, Eko could make some astonishing whistles. His head was built up at the back with a great daub of clay mixed with *punda Mavi* (donkey's dung) into which were inserted several black and white feathers from the cock ostrich. All this decoration made him quite a figure of attraction to the young Turkana Mabibi (maidens).

Eko, in spite of his feathers and mud-pack, which was dyed blue, always looked dusty. His skin did not gleam and apart from cleaning his teeth with a *mswaki* (a natural twig) he avoided water as part of the Turkana tradition. His Kiswahili was very poor and he spoke with an accent as rough as a cat's tongue. He was however an excellent worker, always in good spirits, even when he had nearly severed a toe or finger with his panga and come to me for medical attention. After six months or so, a very dusty Eko came to me and asked for a letter of recommendation as he wanted to join the Kenya Police (GSU). I doubted very much whether he would fit in and I told him so. The poor chap was downcast and asked me to reconsider. He was, he said, prepared for parades and discipline, so I had to relent and sent him off with a good recommendation.

About a year later, a gleaming figure, highly burnished, skin and all, turned up to greet me. One could not have wished for a finer turn-out. His face was alive with happiness and he told me how much he enjoyed life in the Police GSU, and how his people in Turkana would be very impressed when he arrived home.

I had been given a small black mongrel dog by Percy De Batard (a local farmer and member of the Bastard family, in fact a brother of W. K. Bastard who had decided to change his name after several years of adventuring in Canada). I knew that Eko liked the dog: when he was in my employ, he used to take the dog out hunting for birds. So I made him a present of the animal. Many moons later, Eko told me how the mongrel had defended his goats from a marauding leopard in Turkana but in the process, sadly had been killed and eaten by the leopard.

Patrolling the Laikipia plains on foot could be rewarding, for the area was alive with an abundance of small game and bird life. To view, as I did, hundreds of crowned cranes performing their ritual mating dance, crowded together in a congenial gathering, was quite spellbinding.

Once we encountered two buck Thompson's gazelles, their horns locked together in combat, and we were able to walk right up to them, so oblivious were they of anything but their territorial claims, and slap one of them on the rump before they separated and jinked away at top speed.

From time to time, we called upon our very efficient Kenya Police Dog Section. In those days a lot of the dogs came from South Africa, and the commands were given in Afrikaans! In due course locally acquired dogs were enrolled and trained in a variety of skills that included wind scenting, attacking and tracking. The latter was the most important for operational posts. Tracking stolen stock, whether the culprit was Mau Mau or traditional tribal behaviour, across grass plains or in forest areas, was most demanding work for both the dog and his handler. The tracks would be criss-crossed by all manner of game, the scent of which could confuse or entice a dog from his target smell.

One morning, following tracks of a Mau Mau gang which had slaughtered a couple of steers on young Seager Bastard's farm, Sweetwaters, the tracking dog had a hard task, as jackals and hyenas had confused the scent, distracting the animal from the true spoor. I noticed that the handler, John Lockley, whom I met up with many years later at Welkom in the Orange Free State, bent down and appeared to be whispering in the dog's ear every hundred yards or so. At this time I was walking to one side of the main patrol so that I could have a better view of things ahead, in case we flushed any terrorists. I moved across to see what John was up to. To my surprise he had a handkerchief in his hand and was removing grass seeds from the dog's eyes, as they were giving the animal a lot of discomfort. Like the majority of follow-up patrols, this one was uneventful, as the Mau Mau gang made it to the forest, carrying the meat over their shoulders.

Once, 'Young' Seager Bastard (as there was an older Seager Bastard, an uncle on a nearby farm) came roaring down to the police post with a tractor-load of men requesting our assistance. A huge swarm of locusts had settled in his wheat, where I regularly culled the poaching *Kuru* (waterbuck). We turned out all available hands and, along with his farm labourers, waved sacks around in a futile exercise to try and get the locusts to move on. I think that the attendant flight of cranes did more harm to the swarm than our puny efforts but my askaris did return to the post with sacks of locusts that were fried in hot fat and eaten later in the day.

One of my NCOs, Corporal Mumu, a Mkamba, (one of the tribes that made up the bulk of the security forces in those days) was a skilled tracker and, under his tuition, I absorbed some of his teaching. He was quite a smart-looking man, with the arrow-like tattoos just beneath both eyes that are favoured by the Mkamba. He let me follow tracks, both of game and Mau Mau, stopping me when I went wrong, and showing me how to read the sign. I began to learn that following spoor was more a case of watching out for a pattern of changing colours, rather than just printmarks on the ground. Eventually I achieved some level of proficiency and completed a Tracker Combat course.

When we were following tracks of Mau Mau, Corporal Mumu would sometimes stop, bend down and collect a small bundle of grass behind him, then tie the bunch in a knot still without looking behind him. The aim was to put some powerful medicine on the success of the mission. I picked the idea up too. He had another quirk and that was his insistence on cutting out and eating the small intestine of a buck immediately after the kill. This he did alone! But he also showed me how to skin a buck, and then cook the offal on a stick over a quickly-made fire.

I still have nostalgic memories of this, my first group of askaris, and it was a bitter blow when we had to bury, with full police honours, Constable Mutisya, another Mkamba, who was killed in a fierce, but brief exchange of fire with a Mau Mau gang on Minns' Farm in Nanyuki. Mutisya was a large and well-built man who always had a smile on his face. He was well-liked by his colleagues. Even though we administered morphia and got him to hospital within a couple of hours, he quickly succumbed to his bad stomach wound.

For most of 1956–57, the time was spent leading one, and then two tracker combat teams on the lower slopes of the Aberdares, in the Mweiga and Ngobit areas, where 'White Farms' bordered the forest and were therefore subject to stock theft and killings by Mau Mau gangs. Our efforts to combat the threat were largely ineffectual. It was more a case of following up after an incident, sometimes following tracks for half a day or more, but never achieving a satisfactory contact. But life was not monotonous as there was a wide variety of things going on around one in the bush; and living under canvas, when it is not raining, can be invigorating.

On patrol one morning, again along the Uaso Nyiro, but much further west, where the river tumbles off the Aberdares, we put up a cock ostrich which took off in its crazy, swaying run, with its head lurching from side to side, right ahead of us. The bird ran straight into a farm three-strand fence, got entangled, and tore the top of its head clean off. The bird remained upright for a few seconds, blood pumping out of the top of the creature's neck, before collapsing in a dying heap on the ground. The prized white feathers of the cock ostrich were gathered by the grateful Turkana and Samburu members of my team, to be used for personal decoration once they reached their home manyattas.

For a few months the teams camped in the Uaso Nyiro Police Post, Mweiga, which was under the command of Inspector Peter Edwards, a smart and quietly efficient officer, who arranged for us to have the occasional hot bath at the farms of local settlers. Peter and I also spent a night or two sleeping out in a local miniature 'Treetops', that was set in a natural clearing in the Aberdare forest. Equipped with a car battery and floodlamp, we were able to get close-up views of buffalo and other game that ventured within range.

Completely out of the blue and with no form of warning from my Divisional Headquarters, I would receive periodic visits from Major-General Sir Robert Hinde. He would arrive at Bernings, just him and a KAR driver in a Land Rover or Austin

Champ, and we would pore over local maps whilst he probed
into my local knowledge of Mau Mau activities.

Once he arrived as I was tucking into my lunch, curried
kanga; he sat at the table with me, eating his own sandwiches,
having refused my offer of sharing my humble repast. Certainly an unconventional general, someone somewhere had
given him the nickname of 'Looney' Hinde; but he was a most
likeable man and the fact that he spent half an hour with a
humble police inspector, sought my views and experiences and
displayed considerable understanding of the anti Mau Mau
campaign, made his visits both welcome and unpainful.
General Hinde had a brother who farmed in Kenya, and from
his conversation it was easy to gather that he had far better
access to local views, both of the settler and the Kikuyu, than
other senior Army officers.

Now and again on the Laikipia plains, it was possible to
come across an unusual unit in the shape of the Mounted
Section whose riders were a mixture of both regular and KPR
officers. In the Nanyuki area the Mounted Section was led by
Major Hugh Massey, and we did meet up once or twice as they
patrolled the local ranches. One heard stories of them achieving
kills against the Mau Mau whilst on 'moonlight' patrols: but I
have no direct evidence of this.

The contract Inspectors that flooded into Kenya during the
Emergency, known as 'Two Year Wonders' by those that came
before, were from a variety of backgrounds and disciplines.
The majority had some sort of Armed Forces training, which
was to stand them in good stead against the Mau Mau. In
Nanyuki we had Ron Martin, a Rhodesian, who married an
attractive young lady and was the envy of his bachelor
colleagues. At Dol Dol Police Station Paddy Burke held the
reins of command. When on safari, Paddy would criss-cross
from manyatta to manyatta, calling in to have a drink (of milk?)
with every chief or headman that he passed. His police station
had a large stock pound. As the national sport was stock theft,
Paddy always had a large herd of stock awaiting either court
action or reclaiming by the owners. Over the years the animals
in the pound produced offspring, and in time Dol Dol had a

'phantom' herd of stock that belonged to the police station and provided them with fresh milk and meat.

The DTO at Nyeri, one Terry Groves, a Londoner who went on to marry a Bugandan princess, once sent a Land Rover to Nairobi for write-off. When the vehicle was being assessed in Nairobi, it was found to be of a length never produced by Rover. Further examination revealed that it in fact comprised two unequal halves from former wrecks that had been written off in Central Province. Who was behind this master innovation, I have no idea.

There were of course many with the missionary zeal. John Cumber used to refer to them as 'God-botherers' in a light-hearted fashion. In Meru, when Anglican and Church of Scotland churches bordered each other, there were frequently ructions when African converts were caught taking a short cut across the property of the other church. Sometimes their unchristian rivalry became as vehement as their combined denouncement of the Devil.

The Roman Catholic Consulata Mission in Nyeri had a big plantation devoted to growing coffee; indeed the early Consulata staff had helped to pioneer the growing of the crop in Kenya. One day, whilst tracking a Mau Mau gang through the mission's large estate, I was confronted by a very angry Italian priest who attempted to obstruct me. I reminded him that there was an Emergency on and that it was not my intention to enter any buildings without permission from the staff. He reluctantly gave way. A few months later he was much more amenable, when I was called to remove a violent lunatic who had broken into the charnel-house, where he had lit a fire and was making soup from the crushed bones of the dead. The frothing at the mouth lunatic was subdued with the aid of a large blanket, which fortunately also nullified his swinging panga.

I was subsequently invited for tea at the mission, with my hosts being a contingent of American priests. They were much less fanatical about their Kikuyu converts than their Italian counterparts. It was an eye-opener when the Americans produced their considerable arsenal of sporting rifles. Apparently these were bought at diplomatic rates, no taxes needing to be paid, and they were for the most part all avid hunters.

Conversation across the table was along the lines of, 'I crawled to the top of the ridge and took aim (at a buck), after establishing from its sexual organ that it was a male!'

One day on the main Nanyuki–Nairobi road, I met up with a large chap, taller than six foot and heavier than eighteen stone, whose exhaust pipe had parted company from his Morris Traveller. With the aid of some wire and the laces from my jungle boots, the exhaust was returned to place, hopefully to remain there until the next garage. The giant was Ted Evans, MBE, CPM, with whom, some 35 years later on, I was to backpack in the Brecon Beacons. Ted is a good person to have to windward when walking in a gale!

FOUR

PATROLLING MOUNT KENYA

In May, June and July of 1955, the *East African Standard* ran a series of articles on Ndathi Police Post, the post I commanded. The post was sited at about 7,000 feet on the southern slopes of Mount Kenya, above Kiganjo where the Kenya Police Training College is situated. Alongside the post was a large village of Kikuyu, most of whom were employed by the Forestry Department, and the nearby European farms of Messrs Hewlett, Dixon and Walker which were completely encircled by thick forest and known as the 'Island Farms'. The articles noted the successes of the anti Mau Mau patrols and ambushes mounted by the post and also included a letter of commendation from one of the farmers, Malcolm Hewlett, who acted as a spokesman for his two neighbours.

The success of the post largely centred around two very excellent Kikuyu trackers; Gachingiri and Kinyua, both formerly of the Forest Department, workers with a formidable knowledge of tracks, both game and logging, and perhaps the most vital of skills, an uncanny instinct to anticipate where Mau Mau gangs were likely to be heading, even when we had lost sight of their spoor. The trackers were paid from funds received as the result of successful engagements, and there was usually sufficient money remaining to buy them suitable clothing and strong hockey boots for forest patrols. Indeed, due to the lack of official supplies of jungle boots, we also used to buy boots for the askaris. All this came out of the £50 or so that we received for a 'good contact'. Our supplier was an Indian trading store at Kiganjo owned by Mepa.

Apart from the post driver, all the askaris were Kenya Police Reserve; consequently the latter addressed the former as 'Commissioner', a title he revelled in!

Expatriate colleagues with me at various times were the Welshmen John Lewis and Cyril Gillett, the jazz fiend Mike Hudson and the humorous but eccentric Mike Cotten. Prior to my arrival the post had been commanded by Alan Johnson, an Inspector who had himself gained several accolades from the local farmers for his good work. The leading NCO was Sergeant Akwei, a fearless Turkana who led from the front. It was Akwei who instilled in me the benefit of the 'controlled rush' when combating Mau Mau gangs in the exceedingly thick forest, with no signs of fear for his own safety. In fact one of my first tasks was to learn to keep up with the marauding Akwei. Such tactics often resulted in our both coming back with bloody faces caused by the onslaught of branches, as we sped through the undergrowth in top gear.

As was common with most forest posts, Ndathi was constructed by local villagers out of cedar off-cuts, hence looking vaguely like a Wild West log cabin, plus some reinforcement by way of lining the roof with flattened paraffin 'mkebe' (tins), that made it almost watertight during the torrential rains. Furnishings were rough and consisted of items borrowed from farmers, including two ancient African-type trestle beds. In spite of our considerable resourcefulness in furnishing the post from local sources, for many months we fought a continuous battle with the 'accountants' at Police Headquarters, who tried to charge us rent! It is pleasing to record that with our persistent ingenuity, we won!

The 1st Battalion of the Rifle Brigade was stationed just above the Island Farms, commanded by Lt. Col. Peter Hudson (later Lt. Gen. Sir Peter Hudson) who was known as 'Rock' or 'Soapy' by his men. We liaised closely, Peter did several joint patrols and the Battalion assisted us with target practice. The Rifle Brigade were keen, naturally, to achieve some successes against the Mau Mau, and they put out some feelers as to whether they could borrow our trackers.

As the police relationship with the trackers was a very personal one, built up over some time with each knowing the other very well, and since we also exercised considerable care for them and their families after working hours, we could not farm them out to any third party. So as not to cause too much disappointment, I explained to the Rifle Brigade that they could have the assistance of the trackers in a combined patrol, with Police Inspectors commanding the police element, which included the trackers, and the Army officer looking after his own men, with the overall direction of the patrol, route, etc, remaining in the hands of the police. This was agreed, and we did a few joint patrols in the Thego and Nairobi River areas of Mount Kenya.

So on my terms we set out, a patrol of some twenty heavily armed men, about equal proportions Police and Army. On the first patrol we were proceeding cautiously through thick bush, with the trackers casting around for spoor, when I heard a command of 'Halt' some thirty minutes after we commenced walking. When I asked the officer what was going on he replied, 'Jungle Juice,' and I could then see that each soldier had stopped and was pouring himself some lemonade from his water bottle for a quick drink. I was offered some and also told that the juice was very good for cleaning old brass! A radio started up and our position was relayed back to the Army camp; all very efficient but so noisy and out of keeping with our silent routine. It seemed to me that we were not going to achieve very much that day and, I am afraid, we did a lengthy, but mainly routine patrol before homing to our respective bases.

There were also fairly frequent calls from the Army to borrow my long wheelbase Land Rover. At that time the Army in my post vicinity were only equipped with short-base Land Rovers, and I became aware from my driver's reports that our vehicle was being used to ferry soldiers to hospital who had been wounded in firearms accidents, whilst cleaning them and so on, when they needed taking to the nearest military hospital by stretcher.

When we went to the range it was of course a different matter and whatever the target, distance or weapon, the Rifle Brigade were tops. We accepted that as the professional soldiers they were miles ahead of us when it came to small-arms skills. However, on bush patrols I believe we had the edge!

On one occasion we had excellent information that there was a large gang, something in the region of 50 or 60 strong, lying up on the banks of the Nairobi river on the lower slops of Mount Kenya. We mounted a big operation and I was asked by the Rifle Brigade if I would take two or three of their best marksmen along with my patrol: no officers, just NCOs or privates. As the marksmen had clearly demonstrated to me that they could hit anything that moved, I agreed and took three of them with my patrol. I thought that if we had a good contact, then with the addition of accurate fire-power we were likely to achieve better results.

We came on to something almost immediately after we had got into thick undergrowth: there was a small but distinctive mark on a tree indicating to us that there were Mau Mau present. After casting around, the trackers picked up the spoor of two or three people, possibly a feeding party, and we followed a most torturous trail, up and down the steep valleys of various rivers that flow off Mount Kenya, going against the grain of the country, down 300 feet, then up 500 feet, and so on, up and down. In the deep river valleys you could not hear a thing, such was the noise made by the fast-flowing waters. We were climbing almost vertically up an extremely high river bank, almost at the top when it happened.

The strict patrol orders were that one should always try to remain in file; if you had to break file because of an obstruction, then you should not get ahead of the man who was normally ahead of you. As we came over the lip of the valley, after the steep climb, the tracker was in front and I should have been immediately behind him, but one of the marksmen got in front of me and separated me from contact with the tracker, just as the latter almost fell over a Mau Mau sentry who was lying in the grass. What had happened was that we had come into the camp at the lightly guarded rear end. The Mau Mau, not expecting to be approached from the very steep river valley, had posted most of their sentries on the side furthest from us.

As the tracker almost fell over the sentry, letting fly with his shotgun (and missing him), the poor marksman in front fell back with shock right on top of me, his trigger finger on his SLR. Whether the rifle was fully automatic or whether he pulled the trigger several times, I do not know. But the spout of his SLR went past my eyes spitting red and yellow flames, something I can remember to this very day. The noise was deafening and I thought I had been shot. As the marksman fell, so the bullets whizzed past my eyes.

All the Mau Mau escaped and we returned to camp with our tails between our legs, cursing inwardly at our misfortune.

On another day, we were working the area that runs from Ndathi to the Royal Lodge at Sagana and on towards Hombe. The usual thick forest prevailed but was interspersed in some areas with spacious *vleis*. Picking up some tracks in the long grass, we followed them until one of the trackers indicated (by hand sign) that he could see something ahead. I could see what he was pointing at and, as I crawled forward it looked to me like an animal skin, possibly a Mau Mau wearing a hyrax skin coat. Whatever it was, it was motionless and could be asleep. It seemed a golden chance to capture a terrorist alive. Creeping forward, I made a sudden grab for the skin that was now plainly visible. To my surprise, and no doubt his, I grabbed hold of the tail of a wild dog, a black-and-white spotted creature, that yelped wildly and then took off with the rest of the pack that was sleeping in the grass. To hoots of laughter from my patrol, the pack of wild dogs crashed into the forest, truly black and white terrors on four legs.

Contact with Mau Mau gangs was usually a fast and furious affair, the actual engagement being over in a matter of minutes, even though tracking the gang down might have taken half a day or more and, on some occasions, several days. During one six-month period at Ndathi, we accounted for over forty Mau Mau, all except one being 'kills'. In the dense bush, wounded gangsters usually crawled away to die in seclusion, when of course they would be taken care of by the hyenas and other scavengers. It was not unusual to see a dead body covered in a seething mass of *siafu* (safari ants) only a few hours after death, so finger prints or facial photographs had to be taken promptly, or some other arrangement made.

Once we had the frustration of sighting a gang, late one afternoon moving out of the forest on Mount Kenya, crossing an open vleis, and no doubt coming down for food. We counted about twenty of them, but they were at least two miles away and the dead ground between us would have taken several hours to cross. We fired the Bren in their general direction and they high-tailed it back into the cover of the forest.

Carrying out anti Mau Mau patrols in the forests of Mount Kenya and the Aberdares required a good pair of lungs and sturdy legs. The terrain was far from friendly, the bush in parts being extremely thick so that advancement called for the necessity to stick to game tracks or sometimes 'buffalo tunnels'. When scouting for tracks, we patrolled against the grain of the mountain, up and down densely-bushed river gorges, to cover maximum ground and in the process putting considerable strain on the lungs. Mau Mau gangs had learnt from bitter experience not to lay up alongside the busy rivers that tumbled down from the mountains, as the noise of the river would hide the approach of security force patrols.

Big game, mainly buffalo, rhino and elephant, also posed problems. In the early days of the Emergency, their unpredictable actions were exacerbated by the sheer terror caused to all animals by the bombing runs of the RAF Lincolns and Harvards. On some occasions we would be 'treed' by an irate rhino or buffalo. One night, well after dark, we tried to move what we thought was a buffalo from our path by throwing sticks at it. The animal turned out to be an elephant lying down, and being only a few yards from the patrol, it was a great relief for us when the beast decided to wander away. At that time we were in the giant bamboo on Mount Kenya and there were no trees of any kind around.

My expatriate colleague, John 'Taffy' Lewis, and the rest of us spent an extremely cold night dressed merely in paper-thin jungle greens, on the banks of the Waraza River, between 9,000 and 10,000 feet up, surviving a night of abject misery only due to the fact that one of the trackers had a box of matches in his pocket, which enabled us to light a large bamboo fire which we all slept around, turning over from time to time to warm the other side. Such nights out were not common but did occur now and again as we got enthusiastically set on following Mau Mau tracks. I think that on this particular occasion our quarry was crossing the shoulder of Mount Kenya, heading for Nanyuki or perhaps even Meru.

I formed a close relationship with our leading tracker, Kinyua, which extended to helping his immediate family and, as the Emergency eventually called less for his skills, arranging for him to get a good job in the National Parks. We had a good understanding and on patrol seldom needed to talk, usually being fully conversant with signs and motions. One day he indicated that there was 'something' in the clearing ahead. I indicated a general rush, and to our surprise, and that of the beast in question, we ran full pelt at a sleepy old buffalo which fortunately, had the good sense to flee in the other direction. On another patrol Kinyua indicated that he could hear something in the undergrowth ahead. We had just changed places and I had assumed the lead position, when he thrust me to one side and stabbed with his shotgun a gigantic porcupine that was coming down the track at me with its bristles at the high port!

In the Thego River valley on one patrol, it became necessary, due to the density of the bush, to resort to using a buffalo tunnel. These passages through the undergrowth were opened up by the huge boss of the buffalo's horns, closing in behind the beast but leaving an aperture wide enough for a man to crawl through. Not an ideal sort of track to use, for obvious reasons, but sometimes the only way to make noiseless progress. As we had found human signs in the area, there was little point in dallying. The patrol of ten men led by Kinyua started crawling down the tunnel, pushing aside the strands of vine and 'wait-a-bit' thorn that clutched at us. Some ten minutes into our crawl, Kinyua stopped and made sign that there was something ahead. It could possibly be buffalo, but he was not sure! We swapped places and I got Kinyua to move to number three in the patrol, after much cursing and wriggling, so that the Bren gunner was immediately behind me. I made the sign of the *nyati* (buffalo) and indicated that he should fire over my prone figure, should the beast charge. It was very hot, we were thirsty and our mouths dry with anticipation, excitement and fear.

I crawled on, closely followed by an even sweatier Bren

gunner, knowing that his weapon was cocked though the safety catch on. The minutes ticked away as I got nearer to the object, which I could now see was black and looking remarkably like the end of a buffalo boss. Something persuaded my knees to keep digging into the ground as we edged even closer. It came as a shock when, only a few yards away from the black object, my eyes focused on something that now seemed more like a gun barret. I scurried the last few yards as fast as circumstances would permit, grabbed hold of the flash eliminator of a Bren gun that was pointed down the tunnel and in doing so woke up the three British soldiers who were dozing alongside the weapon that was mounted on a bipod. There followed an embarrassing conversation. The soldiers had misread their map, were on the wrong river and could all have been 'chingered' (had their throats cut) had we been Mau Mau. No official report was made by us as I thought the soldiers had been shaken enough already.

Christmas and New Year on operational posts came and went virtually the same as any other day; in the Muslim areas of the Northern Frontier, work went on as normal. There were no special celebrations although sometimes we were lucky enough to receive a well-prepared parcel from the East African Women's League (EAWL), containing a Christmas cake and pudding, plus some paperback books, and so on. The ladies of the EAWL did sterling work which was greatly appreciated by the security forces.

There were post inspections to cope with, which were cause for some concern in a busy operational area as they upset our schedule of forest patrols. We were visited by Colonel Alec K. Doig, District Officer, Kiganjo, along with the Provincial Commissioner, Central Province, which passed off well as the post got a commendation; and by Brigadier Lord Thurlow of the British Army, whom I pressed for some lightweight sleeping bags, so that we could do more in the way of long patrols up to the moorlands of Mount Kenya. The latter did send us a consignment of sleeping bags but they were so big and heavy that they needed to be carried by vehicle!

There came a time when it was necessary to rest our two trackers, Messrs Gachingiri and Kinyua, and give some operational experience to others who were keen to demonstrate their skills and also to earn some extra money. Off we set on patrol one morning, shortly after dawn, heading up Mount Kenya roughly in line with the Sagana River. The patrol was well into the small bamboo and it was early afternoon when the Kikuyu tracker, dressed in a distinctly off-white raincoat, suddenly scuttled to one side and disappeared into the thick clumps of bamboo, followed by the rest of the patrol. Suddenly I was alone. The bush was deathly quiet and I could not hear or see any big game that might account for the sudden scattering of my men. I took the safety-catch off my Sterling and moved slowly along in the general direction that the rest of the patrol had taken.

As I came out of one thick clump of bamboo, I saw an African ahead of me dressed in an old white raincoat. I approached him slowly and, so as not to scare him, when I was a couple of paces away from his rear I whispered, 'Wapi kifaru?' (Where is the rhino?). The African spun round quickly and fell over, in the process dropping his home-made rifle! I told him to stay down. But he was up in a trice and running like a hare when he fell under a short burst from my Sterling.

Hearing the shooting, the rest of the patrol quickly rallied round me and, after a pow-wow and wider search of the area, it was found that we had come upon a Mau Mau camp, without following any tracks. Our trainee tracker had sighted a Mau Mau sentry, panicked and fled, followed by the rest of the patrol who thought they had a contact! We had missed a gang of twenty or more and, for our day's labours, had one Mau Mau sentry and the knowledge that there was nothing to touch the skill and bravery of our two regular trackers.

On the way back home to Ndathi, a lengthy but downhill route, we spoke in a light-hearted manner of the shock the Mau Mau sentry must have had: firstly at being spoken to in Kiswahili, and secondly at having a *mzungu* creeping up behind him. The failed tracker, in an effort to re-establish his stock, offered to remove the honey from a man-made bee-hive that was slung from the uppermost branches of a large tree. Up he went like a honey badger, pausing only when the busy occupants of the hive came out to greet him. He said that he could not get at the honey as the bees were too alert and he had no matches to make smoke. So he undid the wire that held the barrel-like hive to the branch, and let the whole outfit crash to the ground. We all scattered and, as the hive hit the ground with a large crash, angry bees swarmed all over the place, stinging those that had not bothered to take more than a few paces. After the turmoil had died down, we did have a good helping of honey each, spitting out the young immature bees, and then helping to remove the stings from the tracker when he was finally allowed out of the tree by the bees.

Patrols in conjunction with Inspector Mike Marsh, of the Royal Lodge Police Post, were always an interesting diversion from routine. On one such patrol we were checking for tracks, at first light, that may have crossed the Royal Lodge–Ndathi road either into or out of the forest, when Mike spotted a couple of Mau Mau couriers resting with their loads right by the side of the track. By the time we all rushed to his aid, Mike had accounted for both of them, being in fact the only person to spot them though half the patrol had already passed the spot.

On another patrol we ventured into the area of Hombe Police Post, as we were on to some tracks; and being without a radio we poached without permission, which is not a wise thing to do. By mid-morning we had stopped for a rest and, as we lay around in an untidy circle, we could hear some crashing in the undergrowth. As we stood up, a patrol from Hombe Police Post, led by an excited tracker dog, burst in amongst us. They were following tracks too! The day ended amicably, but we were all aware of what might have happened if someone had been eager on the trigger.

On one of the controlled rushes against a Mau Mau gang, Sgt. Akwei took off like a long dog, crashing through the forest in pursuit of a splinter group, with myself on his heels. The two of us soon became isolated from the rest of the patrol as we cornered two of the gangsters in a thicket of tangled vines and thorn bush that they could not extricate themselves from. Both Mau Mau were frantically pulling on the springs of their home-made guns, as they went down under a hail of fire from Sgt. Akwei's Sten. In my anxiety to assist Akwei, I sprayed the bush either side of him, taking my finger off the trigger as his back came into view, but in reality I believe that he got both of the Mau Mau. The fearless Akwei, not one to keep to short bursts, often used up all his ammunition and ended up cracking skulls with the butt of his Sten. Indeed, after one such episode, his damaged Sten butt was welded in a local Kiganjo garage.

On return from one extended absence, I was met by a smiling Cyril (Taffy) Gillett, my post colleague at that time, who told me that the post had been visited by Superintendent 'Paddy' Thompson who had administered a rocket to Taffy as the Post Occurrence Book (OB) was 24 hours behind. The visit took place on a Friday and the last entry in the OB had been for Thursday. Taffy, who has a high falsetto laugh when excited, was beside himself with mirth, as he revealed to me that the last entry in the OB was in fact from the previous week.

A District Officer at Karatina, one John Campbell (John D. Campbell, MC and Bar, OC 'S' Patrol) who had a distinguished record during the Second World War when he served in Popski's Private Army, contacted me one day as he had some good information on local Mau Mau. Even though the area in question was outside my post district, the powers-to-be allowed me to go ahead. One dark night, with a small fighting patrol and in the company of John and his informer, we crept up to an isolated hut on the fringe of the forest and waited for the gang to appear. Nothing happened, so we returned to Karatina. On reaching base, I was eager to see what weapon John had been carrying, for he was immediately behind me in the patrol. He was armed with a cocked Verey pistol that had been captured from the Mau Mau, and had adapted the weapon to fire shotgun cartridges!

The following night Taffy Gillett undertook the same patrol. I had warned him about the Verey pistol and this time the isolated hut did contain some quarry. It was fortunate that Taffy and his men were very careful to issue a challenge, for the hut contained some Kikuyu youths who had been persuaded to ignore the curfew and venture to the forest edge by the informer. The latter was evidently trying to curry favour with the District Officer and, in the convoluted way in which the

Kikuyu mind works, had sent his own kind into grave danger. As it was, the informer got a severe wigging and the Kikuyu youths were escorted back to their village.

Next to the Royal Lodge at Sagana, where I was stationed for a few months, there was a thriving trout hatchery headed by D. F. Smith and his assistant Julian McKeand. As a special favour, D. F. let me cast my line in the breeding pond and reel in some really big trout that were never landed, as we fished with special flies that had no hooks! D. F., as I always addressed him, for I never knew his Christian name, also let me into the secret of the nets that he pulled across the runs below the 'Royal Pool', whenever Royalty was staying at the lodge, to ensure the occupants of a catch. Never one for shooting game, whenever there was need to cull or shoot an injured beast he would call upon Julian to get his 'pipe', his euphemism for a rifle!

FIVE

PSEUDO GANGS IN THE FORESTS OF MOUNT KENYA, ABERDARES, THARAKA AND RIFT VALLEY

After leaving Ndathi Police Post, I went round the mountain to Embu and took over a Special Force team, based in the Keruguya area, from Mike Hudson, a former colleague from Ndathi. Some wag had named the camp 'Kimathi' after the notorious Mau Mau gang leader. Driving alone to the camp, I stopped to ask an Embu *Mzee* (Elder) the way to the camp, which was hidden along a minor road, amongst many other minor roads.

'Jambo mzee, U Hali Gani? Wapi Kimathi?' (Greetings, old man. What is your news? Where is Kimathi?) The old man grinned, said that all was well and hadn't I heard? – Kimathi was dead! – There was no answer to that.

Along with a Field Intelligence Officer (FIO), Steve Stevenson, and the somewhat worn-out Pseudos at Kimathi Camp, we scoured the Embu forests for a gang leader known as 'Mshenzi' (Barbarous), a title he adopted as it appealed to his sense of humour. Something of a local gangster, his robbery and acts of violence were directed solely against his own tribe. In a fit of enthusiasm, we actually captured one of his gang, unwounded. He was a tall, thin man known as 'Gachangichangi' (the beaded one) as he wore many beads. He was run down, bowled over and handcuffed before he could raise his *sime* (sword). It was amusing to watch him stare open-mouthed at my removable, false dreadlocks (not quite as long as his), and he also found my scent upsetting: even though I had not washed for a week or so, he still found the residue of long-gone soap odour distasteful.

Unhappily, during a night ambush in a prohibited area, we also shot a lunatic who, like many of his kind in Kenya, have a tendency to live half wild. The poor soul had no claimable kin and was taken into a local police station to arrange for a death certificate and burial. The drama was not yet over for, en route to the police station and whilst negotiating a hairpin bend on a very slippery mud road, my driver succeeded in turning the Land Rover over! After obtaining some manual assistance from a local village, we were success-ful in righting the vehicle but had a little difficulty in finding the body, which had been flung into the bush as we went over the edge cf the track.

My memories of Kimathi Camp, a wooden barn-like struc-ture with the usual *mbati* roof, are centred around the fact that the place was alive with rats, so much so that after dark, I would lie in my bed potting at rats running in the rafters, a torch strapped to a ·22 rifle. The look on Steve's face and his strangled, 'Bloody hell,' told it all.

In 1957 I was invited to join Ian Henderson's 'Blue Doctor' Pseudo team and my transfer was arranged to Special Branch Headquarters, Nairobi, where I took up residence in 'Mayfield' house that acted as our Operational Headquarters. Here the many *mbutus* (teams or gangs) of former Mau Mau terrorists who had been captured, or who had surrendered, were living under canvas. 'Mayfield' was an old house on the Lower Kabete Road, in the area of Spring Valley. It was somewhat isolated, being well set back from the main road and there was scrubland and a river to the rear. As the place bristled with sinister-looking characters, most of whom had retained their plaited dreadlocks, and well armed with a variety of cutting weapons, we were never bothered by strangers and crime generated from external sources was nil!

At this time 'Blue Doctor' forces were re-grouping in the

aftermath of the 'Hunt for Kimathi' operation which is well covered by the book of the same name by Ian Henderson. Apart from being present when some of the photographs were taken for the book, I had no part in the operation which by all accounts was exciting and nerve-racking as the capture of Dedan Kimathi drew to its climax.

I joined up with Dick Maclachlan, also an Inspector, and there FIOs: Bill Eastbrook, Laurie Pearse and Jim Stephens, these three, of whom Jim remained the longest, were all very young and Kenya-born.

The group's main preoccupation now was the capture of the one remaining senior Mau Mau leader, Stanley Mathenge. (It is a matter of historical interest that both Mathenge and Kimathi were born in the Nyeri District of the Kikuyu Reserve, a district that traditionally has always vied for supremacy with the Kikuyu from Muranga (Fort Hall).) There was no hard evidence as to Mathenge's whereabouts. He had once been a prisoner of Dedan Kimathi in the Aberdares (Nyandarua), but he was unbound by a friendly colleague and allowed to escape, before the vengeful Kimathi had him beaten or worse.

Amongst the 'Blue Doctor' Pseudos, there were several from the Othaya District of Nyeri, who had known Mathenge in the forest. Even after all these years there may be old scores to settle, so I will use their first names only. They were Mwangi, Wacieni, Wacigo and Kimotho, the last allegedly being the last person to see Mathenge in the flesh.

After setting up base camps in the Aberdares, teams of Pseudos were let loose into the forests, acting out the part of Mau Mau gangs, as they sought to find the elusive missing leader. The area of search spread from the Mahiga Location in Muranga, north to Muir's Massive and the Ndaragwa slopes of the Aberdares. These teams were fed and debriefed at rendez-vous points by the European members of the team. Meanwhile, other teams led by the Europeans searched the forest edges and selected areas within the Kikuyu Reserve for signs of active Mau Mau members. These latter teams were all dressed in jungle greens to prevent any embarrassing incidents occurring with other security forces, even though the areas had been

cleared with Central Province Operations Room, headed by
former Indian Army Colonel Eric Hayes-Newington, who held
Kenya Police Reserve rank.

It was widely believed that Mathenge was hiding up in a
dakki (an underground hideout). Several such hideouts had
come to notice. They were simple holes in the ground,
sometimes the hollow left by an uprooted tree, that could be
covered by a piece of *mbati*, itself covered with earth, and a
bush placed over the small entrance. Such hides could easily
escape the notice of the casual glance. It is true to say that
amongst the Pseudos, there were also those that believed
that Mathenge had taken refuge in a *dakki*, which had either
collapsed under RAF bombing or due to natural causes, and
that he had been buried.

The weeks went by and nothing of any substance came
to light that could indicate that Mathenge was hiding up
in either the forest or the Kikuyu Reserve bordering the
Aberdares.

An expatriate working in Gailey and Roberts in Nairobi,
contacted Ian and told him that the firm had a Kikuyu working
for them who knew where Mathenge was hiding! In due course
the Kikuyu was produced and, with him in tow, off we set for
the Nyeri area, setting up our tents at Frost Camp on the
moorlands of the Aberdares, at the top of the Kiandanguru
track. Again teams led by Europeans searched the Reserve
areas whilst Pseudos led themselves in combing the still
'prohibited' forest section.

After a while our friendly Kikuyu persuaded us that we
should shift our operations to an area east of Nyeri, in the
thickly wooded valleys around Kiganjo and, later, between
Nyeri and Karatina. Mac and I took two teams into the Chania
River valley one night and at about 3 a.m., we were ambushed
and came under sustained automatic fire. Hugging the ground
for safety and at the same time shouting out, 'Sisi serakali' (We
are Government) for the fire-power seemed over the top for
Mau Mau, I was somewhat relieved to hear a voice reply,
'Niatia Mwamboko' (What is it?). 'Mwamboko' was a name
given to me by the Pseudos. (It is an energetic Kikuyu dance
that to them was indicative of the way I walk.) We had been led

into our own ambush by an all-Kikuyu planning committee. It was indeed fortunate that no one was hurt. The ambush party of six, all firing Sterlings, had opened up on us at about ten yards' range, expending in the process fifty-odd rounds of 9 millimetre.

To view our next area of concern, I went up in a Cessna piloted by 'Punch' Bearcroft. This was a single engined plane but I have flown with him in a twin-engined job. 'Punch' has a reputation second to none as a bush pilot and he made light of the fact that he has only one hand. We flew south of Nyeri, taking photographs of likely areas where a desperate fugitive might hide up. In particular we were looking for areas of dense bush, not too far away from Kikuyu villages, where a lonely man could be fed.

A fifteen-minute flight was enough for me to run off a film of 35 millimetre, as Punch swooped and banked over the South Nyeri Reserve. We spotted several areas of bush that had tracks meandering through them and, rather pleased with our morning's work, we returned to the Mweiga airstrip where, after paying something towards the cost of the aviation fuel used, the film was sent to Special Branch Headquarters for printing and enlarging. The results, whilst not spectacular, did provide the basis for a plan of our next operation.

As with all patrols in the Kikuyu Reserve, the Pseudos were armed with walking sticks and clubs. The Europeans did take the odd firearm, just in case; but more often than not they were content to carry clubs too. Acting on the evidence provided by the aerial photographs, we commenced a series of patrols, scouring the thick bush for several days. As we were due to enter the thickest part of the thorn bush one day, I decided to take a firearm with me and selected a rather fancy rifle with a telescopic lens. As we commenced the patrol, my leader noticed that I was the only person carrying a firearm, and he relieved me of the weapon, removing the telescopic lens which he handed back to me saying, 'You can point this at them if you are confronted by a terrorist!' and he continued the patrol as the only person carrying a firearm. It had been my intention to operate on the periphery of the patrol, hoping to get a pot-shot at anyone that was flushed out. After a week or so we withdrew from the area, I suspect much to the relief of the local Special Branch, and returned to Nairobi.

Late one night just as I was going to bed, Tim Trafford, a Chief Inspector of Nairobi Area Special Branch, came to 'Mayfield' and, after confirming that I had a bottle of whisky handy, he told me that he had reliable information that the friendly Kikuyu who was leading us in the search for Stanley Mathenge, was in fact fabricating a series of events and leading us on a wild-goose chase. I think Tim was right and it was subsequently proved, to our satisfaction, that this was so. The tracks in the thick bush were in fact paths where the local Kikuyu villagers went to set their game traps.

Mac and myself then embarked on a week-long safari into the Samburu Reserve in the Kirimun and Sukuta Marmar areas. We had in tow two captured Mau Mau who said they had information on a gang operating within the Samburu Reserve. Off we went with a couple of Land Rovers and some Pseudos, with orders not to inform the local authorities as Samburu was not a Mau Mau area. With the two Mau Mau handcuffed to the Pseudos as they were not trusted, we walked the Samburu countryside for six days and nights with hardly any food and virtually cat-napping when we could. Apart from being charged by some bad-tempered rhinos, when the handicapped Pseudos had a great time deciding which side of the tree they should run, we found nothing.

We were in and out of Samburu before the local authorities learned of our presence. As we had been poaching again, albeit under orders, Mac and I took the precaution of changing the number plates on our two Land Rovers. We had taken a couple of Samburu, with Kikuyu blood in them, into temporary custody 'to assist with enquiries' but everyone had been well treated and fed on what little we ourselves had been able to acquire from friendly Samburu. Mac and I drove out of Samburu along the stock route into Rumuruti. We were not really fit to drive and kept on dozing off, so a Pseudo was nominated to dig us in the ribs, whenever he saw us nodding. It is the only time in my life that I thought I saw, as I was driving and dozing, a dragon!

Back at De Batard's police post we handed the two Mau Mau

over to the two Nanyuki FIOs, one of whom was Phil Thoms. They returned to Samburu with the two prisoners and, being more trusting, let the two sleep between them unhandcuffed. When the two awoke in the morning, the two Mau Mau had flown.

Several weeks later, when we were busy with other things, Police Headquarters received an official complaint from the Samburu authorities, stating that plain clothes police personnel from another area had been working without permission in the Samburu Reserve. As the vehicle numbers supplied in the complaint were those of two Nairobi Airport fire engines the alleged intrusion was not held against us. We were in the wrong, but we were acting on orders.

On a different occasion, when 'Blue Doctor' Pseudos were operating in the Ol Kalou and Ol Joro Orok districts, concentrating on the numerous small pockets of forest, with myself as the only European, I was approached by a senior government servant and a white farmer and asked if I could do something about a farm-hand who was very active as a passive member of the Mau Mau. When offering to take the chap away for questioning by my men, I was just a little surprised to hear them say that they had something else in mind. I extracted myself from the meeting and took no action, other than to avoid the two gentlemen in the months ahead.

It was not a bad life managing Pseudo teams whether in the Treetops salient or the adjoining areas of the Mwathe or Ruthaithi. Once we dropped teams off, we would have no contact with them until they arrived at a prearranged rendezvous, either for de-briefing or to collect fresh rations. Tins of bully beef left buried in the ground with a marker on top were not always safe. Hyenas have a marvellous sense of smell, and their teeth are quite capable of chewing a corned beef tin to shreds. Camping on the moorlands of the Aberdares at the Frost Camp site, where there was an abundance of water, there was still the journey to make into Nyeri, to collect fresh water in a large and unwieldy water trailer. Ian would not drink the water from the streams or tarns; neither would he touch an egg with a trace of blood in it. It's surprising what you notice when camping! During the rains I drove alone into Nyeri one day to fill up the water trailer. It poured with rain and, whilst trying to climb the National Park track back to the moorlands, the Land Rover did a 180° turn, and there we were sliding down the mountain with several hundred pounds weight pushing the vehicle until it slithered into a ditch...

The call of the *Ngima* (Sykes monkey) first thing in the morning, its deep-throated cry echoing around the forest treetops, and the evening cries of the black and white colobus are memorable. Overhead were martial and black crested eagles, and on the ground more big game than was sometimes comfortable.

A GSU officer, Dick Owen, had been killed, in the Treetops salient in 1955, when he literally crawled onto a rhino which reared up and inflicted a grievous wound in his thigh. He died virtually on the spot from a massive loss of blood. As so often happens, I had met Dick a few days previously and had a drink with him. He was well respected amongst the Island Farm farmers.

Mike Tighe and I were driving up the National Park track one morning, and we had just negotiated a sharp bend, nearly hitting a rhino up the backside, when the beast spun round on a sixpence, stuck his horn under the bumper and lifted the Land Rover off the deck! Mike opened the door of the vehicle, but I grabbed his arm and told him to stay. The rhino became bored and left us with a few scratch marks on the bumper.

I can remember several encounters, on foot, with the unpredictable and bad-tempered rhino whilst stationed at Ndathi and working the Mount Kenya forests. The most serious occasion occurred in an area short on trees. The rhino heard or smelt us from a distance and the creature came thundering along, snorting from both ends, and was on us before we sighted it. The rhino caught one Mkamba askari and had him on the ground, trying to get its horn into him. The askari curled up and made himself into a compact ball. Fortunately, one of the patrol fired over the rhino's head and the beast snorted and then ran off. The askari's trousers were wet with slime from the rhino's mouth where the beast unsuccessfully tried to hook him. There was much jubilation in the post that evening and the askari in question was duly nicknamed 'Bwana Kifaru' (Mr Rhino).

As a by-product of our operations, there was the recovery of elephant tusks and in the Aberdares the Pseudos collected a considerable number of low-grade ivory, usually from elephants that had died of natural causes (we thought!). As mountain elephants are smaller than their plains counterparts, so were the tusks. Once we recovered three tusks at the bottom of a small waterfall. The Pseudos with me suggested that the elephants had been swept over the falls during a heavy downpour, and that one tusk had gone further downstream. As I had seen an elephant come down the flooded Nanyuki river during a violent rain storm, this sounded quite a reasonable hypothesis. I can well remember Ian arranging the return of the collection of ivory, which until then had rested in the hollow bottom of one of the settees at 'Mayfield', to the Game Department.

The Pseudos that formed the Blue Doctor teams ranged from a maximum of 70 running down to about 20 as the call for their skills became less. Not at all talkative to us non-Kikuyu speakers, they did, after I had served with them some time, open up more to me. In the final year or so when I was the only European with the team, they became quite friendly and even provided me with postal addresses so that I could contact them in the future. In fact after the teams were disbanded, I did meet up with some of them in places as far apart as Meru, where Mwangi Mathai was working as a butcher, to Naivasha and Nandi Hills. In the latter I found a former senior member of our team working as a cleaner in the police station. (I was holding a court of enquiry into the alleged misbehaviour of a Police Inspector.) His eyes told me not to recognise or speak to him until we were alone, when we did have a few whispered greetings but the cleaner was adamant that he was content and needed no assistance.

When alone with the Pseudos in the forest, they would relate tales of their experiences as members of various Mau Mau *mbutus* (gangs). One day on the moorlands of the Aberdares, they were watching from a safe distance members of the British Army who were camped there. They saw a 'Tommy' go to the latrine and then return to his camp some thirty yards away. One of the Mau Mau noticed that the Tommy had left his camouflage jacket in the latrine, so he crawled to the structure and pinched it. The amusing part was when the Tommy returned a few minutes afterwards, looking for his jacket, the puzzlement on his face and the scratching of his head had the whole *mbutu* rolling on the ground.

There was fun to be had in the forest. 'Mac' (Dick Maclachlan) did not have very good eyesight: he wore thick glasses and had a tendency to stumble in the bush. Some of the Pseudos would now and again shout out, 'Rhino,' as a startled bushbuck or a bongo crashed away, and then have a good laugh as Mac tore off to seek a tree. Mac in fact was quite a talented medical man. I think he must have had training in the first aid sphere, whilst doing his National Service. He would administer medicine of a bewildering variety, to cure all manner of ailments; he did so with a confident manner and it was his confidence that won the hearts of the Pseudos. At 'Mayfield', Mac had a comprehensive dispensary. He would fill up one-gallon jars at the nearest Health Centre, and then administer Mystic–Spec or some other concoction to calm a sick man. Mac also handled a syringe with expertise and, as the African swears by injections, 'Na safisha damu' (cleans the blood), he always had a stream of willing clients.

Whilst not exactly a bush mechanic, Mac never threw what he termed as 'useful items' away. He had a great collection of such bits and pieces, which must have been put to good use when he retired from the police and opened a hardware store in the Nairobi suburb of Westlands, where he tragically died in 1968. At one time Mac was a Special Branch officer at the Langata Mau Mau Detention Camp, and it is interesting to note that Josiah Mwangi Kariuki, in his book, 'Mau Mau Detainee', written from the other side of the fence, says,

There was one quiet European officer, with moustaches (sic), who seemed very clever and intelligent. He would come and tell us that he did not believe in beating people but that sooner or later, one by one, everyone would confess what he had done. He was a Scot and seemed to have an air of knowing what the future would bring forth. We knew his name was Maclachlan because the loud-speakers were always calling him to go somewhere.

Late one evening whilst camped in a forested area east of the Nyeri–Mweiga road, we had a 'Game Ranger' sign on the main road entrance but we removed the sign after several local farmers came to seek our help in dealing with troublesome game. I shot a green pigeon with a ·22 and was roasting it over a wood fire, when Ian insisted that the pigeon was a poisonous variety and that no one else would eat it. I was stubborn and, having gone this far, was keen to eat the bird. I questioned the Pseudos, all of whom had been well briefed, and I was just on the point of deciding whether to risk eating the bird or sacrificing both the bird and my pride, when I caught sight of Ian grinning. I ate the bird which was surprisingly tasty. Later, after dark, some guinea-fowl came to roost in the trees above our tents. Thinking this was my lucky day, I persuaded one bird to fall out of the tree with a crash into the undergrowth, and then spent a fruitless half an hour looking for the fowl by torchlight.

Apart from big game, there were other 'incidents' that could cause the blood to race. One of the more common was the sudden explosive take-off of the Jackson's francolin, an olive-brown partridge with red bill, feet and toes. The bird would wait until the last moment before taking flight and the eruption from so near by caused the heart to beat faster.

The minute hairs on bamboo caused great itching; but the build-up of gases within the bamboo and the sudden explosion did set the pulse racing as anxious eyes searched the surrounding area for the source of the 'gunfire'! The big bamboo actually contains a lot of water and I suppose that *in extremis*, one could always drink it; but the taste is foul.

Walking across the moorlands and stepping over the many small channels that drain the water into tarns, I was astonished once to see a flash of silver to my side, in water only three or four inches deep. Lying down on my stomach and keeping perfectly still, I saw a large trout moving slowly along the narrow channel, its tail flicking the black peat-like soil on the bottom. As it drew level with me, I scooped the fish out with my hand and estimated that it was about two pounds in weight. Cooked in a frying pan with butter over a wood fire, the trout was delicious.

Time and time again, we would return to the site of the wrecks of the three RAF Harvard light bombers, that followed the leader in a swoop over the bamboo area of the Aberdares, above Nyeri, all three failing to pull out. The Harvards, which I think came from Rhodesia, were visited to see if any inquisitive Mau Mau had salvaged any wire for their game traps; but I think that after initial inquisitiveness, they tended to boycott the area, perhaps thinking that the wrecks were still booby-trapped. Several years after the crash, the tyres on the landing wheels were still fully inflated.

The Pseudos prized the skins of various animals, to be turned into jackets, trousers and hats. They trapped otters, squirrels, suni (a pygmy antelope) and the ubiquitous bushbuck and tree hyrax. The latter, although a very small creature, has a most blood-curdling cry, and sleeping under a tree in which they have their homes can lead to much sleeplessness. If they were lucky, there was also the possibility of trapping something more exotic, such as a honey badger or even the prized leopard. Although very shy creatures, we did catch sight of leopards, on one occasion with two small cubs, which led to much spitting by the mother and some backward steps by us. Once, whilst lying up in a hide, we witnessed the indignity of a leopard being chased away from a beehive by a very fierce honey badger.

When pickings on the Aberdares became even slimmer, we shifted operations towards the northern grazing area, a large slice of country lying to the west of the Nyambenis. Our first incursion comprised the whole Blue Doctor outfit led by Ian. We motored across country, a convoy of some ten vehicles, across vast tracts of unpopulated land (although it was possible to identify old Somali and Samburu manyattas) getting stuck in dry *lugaas* and finding our way blocked by impassable ditches. We eventually set up camp just before dark.

Cpl. Mumu

Blue Doctor Pseudos

Author with his
Combat Tracker
Team

Blue Doctor Pseudo
operations in Tharaka

Blue Doctor Pseudo
operations in Tharaka

Author with Kikuyu
Trackers Gachingiri and
Kinyua (Courtesy of East
African Standard)

Wedding Group Eldoret 9th
April 1966, Best Man
Superintendent Dougie
Hughes of Special Branch

John Loving, Jerry Goodman,
Fred Mason and John Atkinson

Wedding guests and Police
colleagues Harry Jassey,
Parminder Baraj and Des Mair

Author and Major Maingi planning the route of 6,000 head of cattle in the NFD under 'Operation Cowboy'. (Courtesy of John Perry and the Daily Telegraph)

Author as NFD Divisional Commander

Roy McFarlane, Special Branch colleague and fellow footballer with the author

Muharraq Police Station, Bahrain, after a successful haul of National Liberation Front (NLF) bomb making equipment. Bomb Disposal Officer (BDO), Mohamed Aziz, BDO, Brian Shore, Ian Henderson, Yousif Ishaq, Abdul Rahman bu Ali and author

Wing Commander 'Pip' Travell, DFC, taking off from the Police Fort, Manama with his brother Bob aside the Scout on the ground

Sunset Parade at Manama Fort

Author as Deputy Head of Lesotho Special Branch

George Gray (Father-in-Law), author and Jenny, being entertained by the physical fitness group 'Varzesh Bastani' at the International Dept. of the Bank Melli, Tehran

Mountain track to Semongkong (Lesotho)

Senior Government officials bidding farewell to King Moshoeshoe II at Maseru Airport

On safari (trekking and dug-out canoe) with daughter Nicky in the Okavango Delta

Daughter Nicky's Passing Out Parade at Hendon Police College with sister Wendy, Grandfather George Gray, author and wife Jenny

Author as Deputy Head of Special Branch, Botswana

The next morning patrols were sent out with several days' supplies and water. The area was being combed for residue Mau Mau gangs from the Meru district, whom the local Special Branch thought might be operating there. There was very little water, and what little there was, was badly polluted by baboons. So drums of water were secreted at various isolated locations so that our mbutus could replenish their supplies. It was hard country in which to walk, and some of the short, stubby Kikuyu suffered badly from heat exhaustion casting apologetic glances at me when they lagged behind.

One night we were sleeping out in the open – no tents, just a blanket – when we clearly saw one of the Vanguard satellites crossing the sky. I asked Ian whether he would explain to the teams that such satellites sometimes carried monkeys or dogs. He laughed and said that he would prefer not to get embroiled in such a story, as they would not think it true.

After a week or two, Ian returned to Nairobi and left myself and Mike Tighe (FIO) to carry on the task and in particular to concentrate on the foothills that ran along the south-eastern border of the grazing area. Our base camp was set up on high ground alongside a stream that cuts the Isiolo–Nanyuki road, some four miles from the Isiolo boma. Near our campsite were some rusty remains of KAR vehicles which had been swept downstream and wrecked when the quiet stream was suddenly hit by a flash flood some years previously. We worked the area for several months but found no signs of any human activity, other than poachers. The Meru authorities had lain a water pipe through the Grazing Area so that when permission was given for cattle to graze there, water tanks for the stock could be filled. Some wandering Samburu had discovered that the pipe was plastic and that, by sticking a spear in the discernible line of the pipe, they were rewarded by a large jet of what, to them, must have been sweet water.

One morning, after having put a team of Pseudos into the Mount Kenya forest, well above Nanyuki sawmills, I decided not to return to our base in Nairobi. Instead I got one of the drivers to let me off with my kit and I spent three nights alone in the forest, partly for the hell of it, and also because at that time I

was bored with the capital. Armed, and with a lightweight
sleeping-bag and rations, I made myself a small bivouac and
settled down to see what I could observe. The area was alive
with big game so I urinated around the site which, apart from
one night when a herd of elephant got too close and I had to
light up a ndege, served me well. The excitement came about 2
a.m. one morning, when some stealthy rustling set my nerves
on edge. I was in an unzipped sleeping-bag, as past experience
of trying to escape from an inquisitive rhino, zipped up in a bag
and engaging in a sack race through brambles, had been well
digested. As I moved to take the safety-catch off my cocked
Sterling, the rustling stopped and then started again. It was
pitch-black but my imagination could picture a bush-wise
terrorist creeping up for an easy kill. As the noise was getting
closer and my nerves becoming more jumpy, I decided to
throw in my hand. I switched on my small torch and with the
other hand swung the Sterling round to the source of the noise,
to see a large cane rat dragging away a packet of my rations!

In 1978, whilst on holiday in Kenya with my family, we
travelled up from Mombasa to Nairobi on the overnight train.
My wife Jenny and our young daughters Nicky and Wendy
shared one compartment, whilst I was allocated another to
share with a stranger. My travelling companion arrived and
introduced himself as 'Mathenge', the KANU member for
South Nyeri! He said that he had heard from the Kikuyu
bedding attendant that I spoke a little of their language
(Kikuyu). Where had I picked this up? As a farm manager in
Nanyuki, I replied, and was then able to tell him all about Ol
Pejeta Ranching Company, Devon crossed with Boran steers,
and the owner, or leading director, Wickham Boynton. Mathenge
appeared convinced by my farming pedigree and left to have
dinner with friends. Should I have told him that I once spent
many weeks trying to hunt down one of his relatives? Or
perhaps asked him, 'Whatever happened to Stanley?'

Although I had visited the site where the Kikuyu Home Guards
had shot and later on captured Dedan Kimathi, to take a
photograph, I had never seen anything other than a picture of

the 'leader' of the Mau Mau. My young brother Raymond, who served in the Kenya Police on contract for a couple of years, had more luck.

Les Pridgeon, the police officer of the Central Province, told Ray one day, 'I am sending you to prison!' He was one of the European Inspectors nominated to guard Kimathi in a cell at Nyeri Prison before the trial. The European Inspectors did six-hour shifts, one inside the cell with Kimathi and the other on patrol in the corridor. The cell was small and contained a cork-lined table on which there was a basin and water-jug, and a comfortable chair for the Inspector.

Initially, Kimathi had one hand manacled to the wall above the bed but as this caused him some discomfort the doctor suggested that the manacle be fastened lower down, to the bed, and this was done. His leg wound was dressed daily, but still smelt. Kimathi used a chamber-pot in the cell and this, combined with infrequent washing, led to a noticeable odour. The prisoner was talkative and he asked the various Inspectors where they had been stationed. Ray said at Hombe which drew some tales from Kimathi of his brief life in the Mau Mau on Mount Kenya.

Kimathi, who was interviewed periodically by Special Branch, told the Inspectors on guard that he had in fact strangled Stanley Mathenge, as the latter was getting above himself, and that he had also hidden some of the Mau Mau weapons for his own use.

Returning to Frost Camp at the top of the Kiandanguru track one day, I found Ian in conversation with the Director of Intelligence, John V. Prendergast, GM. (Sir John Prendergast, he was subsequently Head of Intelligence in Cyprus, Director of Intelligence in Aden and then headed the Commission against Corruption in Hong Kong.) I joined them. The Director told me that it was becoming increasingly more difficult to renew police contracts. I was on my third, and that he recommended that I should switch to permanent and pensionable terms. The eloquence of the Director convinced me that this was the right course of action and I enlisted his aid in trying to have my pensionable service backdated seven years, as I would be willing to refund the gratuities that I had been paid. Unfortunately, the Ministry of Finance would not countenance the refund I had suggested and I signed on, losing valuable pensionable years in the process. Such is the immaturity of youth!

Blue Doctor teams commenced Pseudo gang operations in Meru, mainly in the Lower Tharaka area, in 1957 and continued with some short spells elsewhere up to 1959 as Mau Mau targets in the forests of Mount Kenya and the Aberdares became sparse. There was indeed a small gang of Mau Mau operating in isolation in the Treetops salient, on the lower slopes of the Aberdares, who were glimpsed from time to time. But as they did not present any security problem and had gone completely 'bush', if not a little mad, and seldom contacted local Kikuyu villagers, they were left alone.

In Tharaka there was a gang leader named Achole, who earlier in the Emergency had been involved in the killing of a nun, at a local Missionary station. In 1957, he had a gang of some twenty-five Mau Mau, all Meru, who existed with the co-operation of local villagers, who were too scared to report on them as they feared retribution in an area that was isolated and seldom visited by the forces of law and order.

Achole and his gang did not remain together as one group but split into smaller gangs, basing themselves in isolated forested areas where they could get food delivered by passive Mau Mau from the nearest village. They did commit robberies and acts of terrorism; but much of what they did was not reported to the police and virtually all the crime was against their own people. In fact as terrorists go, they were largely ineffectual and, in the eyes of the security forces, they were more of a nuisance than anything else.

A Blue Doctor team, some twenty-five in number, moved into Lower Tharaka and set up a base camp. The operation was initially under the command (in the field) of Inspector Richard Maclachlan (who, because of his moustache, was known as 'Charubu' to the Pseudos) supported by myself and Mike Tighe. After a while Mac moved on to other things in Nairobi, to be followed there a few months later by Mike, leaving me to run the outfit on the ground but under the overall command of

Senior Superintendent Ian Henderson, the founder of the Blue Doctor unit.

Unlike the forests of Mount Kenya and the Aberdares, Lower Tharaka was populated, albeit sparsely, so the Pseudos had to operate in jungle greens to help rule out any accidents with the local police and administration, who were aware of our presence. This gave me the opportunity to accompany the Pseudos on various patrols and ambushes and we shared some exciting times together.

Operating in such conditions with Pseudos who themselves had been back in 'civilisation' for some time, meant that they had largely lost the edge which they had originally possessed when they first came out of the forest. Nevertheless, we did have a few successes, including the capture in August 1958, of two of the Achole gang who were completely unarmed: in fact they were 'run down and tumbled over'. They were then 'turned', and joined us in hunting their former colleagues.

Working so far away from my base in Nairobi, I had to depend a lot on local assistance from my colleagues in Special Branch and, in particular, Ted Casey, Alan Thompson and Norman Moore. Sometimes I had the luxury of dining with Pam and Norman Moore at their home in Meru. I can recall having supper with them one evening and showing Pam the vitamin supplement that I took whilst in the bush, because of my poor diet. I was absolutely floored when the pregnant Pam, an ex-Rodean girl, produced identical pills which her doctor had advised her to take!

Prior to each operation in Meru, I went to see the District Commissioner, John Cumber, known as 'Bwana Splendid' because of his use of the latter word. He was a good man to deal with and free of any petty pride that sometimes bedevilled relations between the police and administration. John Cumber had a good career and he went on to be knighted; but he never lost his easy manner and I can recall exchanging letters with him when he was Director-General of the Save the Children Fund.

The Lower Tharaka area was full of tsetse fly and we found these persistent biters extremely troublesome. There was a tsetse research station manned by Larry Wateridge who, incidentally, incurred the wrath of Joy Adamson when he set traps for monkeys in pursuit of his research. Larry wore the same medal ribbons as myself, as he had also served in the Korean theatre. My memories of the tsetse fly are painful. The things would settle silently and bite through all manner of clothing. The bites would come up as hard lumps on the skin. The tsetse is a fast flyer and I always likened them to a jet. When travelling in a vehicle, in spite of the heat, it was far safer to ride with the Land Rover windows closed; than invite the attention of the tsetse, who would otherwise zoom in through the window and quickly select a succulent limb to attack. Travelling in the Aberdeen was another matter, as the cut-away doors and windows afforded plenty of space for silent intrusion.

On one morning I was accompanied by Mike Tighe, a FIO with the Kenya Regiment, the only other operational European with the Pseudos at that time. Mike was feeling a little grumpy that morning and he had hardly muttered more than a couple of words in as many hours. So, when a tsetse fly zoomed into the Aberdeen and settled on his neck, I did not immediately warn him and I therefore felt somewhat ashamed when Mike cried out in pain as the tsetse bit him! We were all bitten many times but to the best of my knowledge none of the group went down with trypanosomiasis or sleeping sickness, although I did spend a week confined to bed in the Inspectors' Mess at Meru, suffering from some unknown complaint that left me listless and feeling sorry for myself.

Down in this part of the world I also had my first introduction to the 'Njuri Njeki', a gathering of Meru elders whose extent of painted face markings reflected their seniority within the organisation. They sat around in a circle, drank *pombe* (beer) and discussed their problems. They held their meetings openly, in a clearing. I was lucky enough to sit in on one meeting and, with the aid of an interpreter, follow the proceedings which, even so, were not always clear to me.

On another occasion we were camped in the Nyambeni Hills, during the rainy season. Well, it rained alright: we had something like 37 inches in one month, quite exceptional and the resultant floods took out most bridges and rendered the main road to Nanyuki impassable. After much scouting around, and aided by the local knowledge of some of the inhabitants, we got four Land Rovers, hitched up together, into Meru. Here we used an old logging track to climb above the town, where we used several old grass tracks to cut back onto the main road, several miles outside of Meru. Even then, we had to seek the assistance of a council tractor to negotiate one stretch that had turned into a quagmire. The Aberdeen was left behind until the roads were opened again.

Camping during these exceptional rains was not comfy. I had a portable camp-bed in the base camp with a ground clearance of eighteen inches. The whole area was water-logged and getting into bed resulted in you and the bedding being submerged. In fact the only really dry place was in the cab of the Land Rover or up a tree

During my time in Tharaka, several incidents occurred which were unusual. The first happened when one of my Pseudos, whose name was Gacharu, known to his compatriots as 'Mura wa Gachaha' (son of Gachaha), and who hailed from the Kagongo Location (Location 19) of Fort Hall (Muranga), was unlucky enough to contract a very bad dose of cerebral malaria. For his own safety he had to be restrained in handcuffs, as there was a danger that he might throw himself into a river or do some himself some other form of injury. There was also the possibility that he might harm others, as he was a short, hefty man who could swing a panga or sime (sword) with some verve. We were in the middle of an operation in Lower Tharaka, and some walking distance from our base camp, when Gacharu fled away from our hide one night. He was pursued to the banks of the Ura river where we cornered him and wrestled him to the ground, as he was trying to brain himself on some large boulders. He was sedated until daybreak, when we retraced our tracks back to base camp, strapped him in the front seat of a Land Rover, and drove to Meru hospital.

At the time we thought Gacharu had gone mad, until the doctor diagnosed a particularly virulent strain of cerebral malaria. All the team were taking anti-malarial tablets, and it would seem that poor old Gacharu was just unlucky. He remained in hospital for several weeks and became something of a celebrity because of his Mau Mau dreadlocks. On his release from hospital, we took him back to Fort Hall and discharged him from the Pseudo team. From time to time, we would call in to see Gacharu in Location 19. He was always pleased to see us and we usually left items of food for him and his family. It was unfortunate that he never really recovered from his attack of malaria and his brain remained affected by the disease.

On another occasion, whilst attempting to cross the Thangathia River, not far from its junction with the Tana, we became firmly stuck on a sandbank. I was driving a $1^1/_2$ ton Aberdeen lorry, a police vehicle with a caged back, twin rear wheels and a huge carrying capacity. Not very good in mud and devoid of side doors, the Aberdeen's cut-away body enabled one to disembark quickly but also, of course, let the rain in when the heavens opened. Although there were about ten of us, we could not shift the wretched lorry, and I can recall to this day keeping an anxious eye on the sky, as I could visualise it raining heavily and the whole outfit being swept downstream by the bore and having to submit a length loss report!

Fortunately, none of these things happened. I knew there was a district officer named Bob McConnel, stationed in Tharaka, and we promptly dispatched a runner to request a Land Rover to pull us out. In a couple of days, Bob arrived and the Aberdeen was pulled onto dry land. Whilst we were awaiting his arrival, we did some fishing and shot some game birds for the pot using a ·22 rifle that made very little noise. When wading bare-footed in the river, the catfish would come and nibble the bottoms of our feet. The river also contained some very large eels, one of which I caught and was trying to land, when a Pseudo rushed up with his panga and cut the line, shouting that we did not want a dangerous snake among us!

We brewed up on Bob's arrival and exchanged news of local events as we sat drinking tea made from the boiled waters of the Thangathia which, if one thought about it, had passed through several villages before reaching us. Bob was an introspective person who, later on, spent several years on the bleak shores of Lake Turkana, whence he emerged positively bleached white, having been working with the fishing industry there.

*

Large-scale maps of the Lower Tharaka area were difficult to come by, and those that came my way from the Police Headquarters Operations Room were frequently stamped 'area obscured by cloud', and so detail did not show up on aerial survey. The Ops Room were able to drum up some local maps from the Surveys Department which had been drawn by District Officers stationed in the area and, rather embarrassingly, I was asked to let them know of any additions or alterations that I came across so that the Survey Department could be informed. Whilst not my strong point, I did pass on a few local names of minor hills and forested areas to the Chief Inspector running the Operations Room.

The latter was always asking me the name allocated to the next operation that I was planning, not being content with the title 'Blue Doctor'. I told him to use any name he liked. On my next visit to the Ops Room I shuddered on seeing that he had written 'Franklin Force' in large letters across the talc covering the Tharaka area.

On pulling out of that area for good, I duly reported to Ian in Nairobi and, as my arrival was well outside office hours, I went to his home in Riverside Drive. He received me warmly and asked whether I had received his personal signal of congratulations. I said that I had, along with one from Colonel Hayes-Newington, the Kenya Police Reserve Officer in charge of the Central Province Operations Room in Nyeri.

Ian went on to say that he was so pleased with the Blue Doctor team's performance under my command that he was recommending me for the George Medal! To support the recommendation he wanted me to write out a list of all the incidents in which I had been personally involved, where there had been direct contact with Mau Mau. I was rather taken aback, surprised and, to be truthful, elated. I did point out, however, that if I was being recommended for an award, then surely it was not up to me to provide the supporting evidence. Ian said that it would help and that I should seriously think about writing the details down. He added that at this stage of the Emergency, I might have to be content with a Colonial Police Medal (CPM) for Gallantry. I went away to ponder.

We met up again in the office a few days later. Ian said that he had submitted the recommendation for an award, even though I had not provided him with the written details that he had asked for. He would show me the letter of recommendation later as he had left the copy at home. A couple of days later I had occasion to call again at Riverside Drive and made so bold as to be shown the letter in question. Ian disappeared into his house for a few minutes, then reappeared to tell me that the document in question was in his office! Neither of us ever referred to the topic again. Did I deserve an award? No!

Lower Tharaka was an area alive with termites and when camping one had to be particularly careful not to place any unprotected items on the ground. The Pseudos cut branches from one of the trees that were iron-hard and apparently termite resistant, and made small trestle tables that were used in the base camp and hides, where one could safely place haversacks and so on. They made me a very superior walking-stick out of the same wood that is with me today and has travelled with me to many other countries.

Sleeping in a hide one night along with a dozen Pseudos, small pieces of canvas draped over trestle sticks in an inverted 'V' shape that protected one from the heavens only, I was conscious of some movement and general restlessness as we lay under our one-man bivouacs. I then felt a weight moving across my legs. Along with my colleagues, and two Tharakan tribesmen who were assisting us, we all turned to with much alarm and as much agility as our sleepy condition would allow and, by the light of a torch, got to grips with a fourteen-foot rock python that was causing mayhem. With a few panga slashes and a couple of arrows from the Tharakans, the snake was killed. The Tharakans told me that rock pythons were plentiful in the area, something we were not particularly keen to hear, and that they usually shot them with poisoned arrows. On this occasion they had used arrows with vicious iron barbed tips. The skin was cured by Zimmerman of Nairobi, and is still with me.

We were also bothered by mambas and cobras and there were numerous occasions when Pseudos were attacked by spitting cobras. Before embarking on the Tharaka operation, I had attended a short course on the treatment of snake bites at the Queen Elizabeth Hospital in Nairobi. I was equipped with syringes and various types of anti snake-bite serum, some of which was supposed to be kept under refrigeration. In the bush I kept the serum in a *sufuria* (cooking pan) of tepid water and hoped for the best. I am not keen on giving injections and at first I was rather apprehensive about the whole issue. However, when someone is bitten and thinks you can save them, then to appear hesitant would be a devastating blow to their morale, so I went ahead, plunging the needle in and hoping that I had the right serum. No one turned their toes up and thanks to the general hardy health of my men, they managed to survive the holes that I made in them.

Spitting cobras sometimes found their mark and succeeded in spraying the faces of the Pseudos. I had not received any instruction from the hospital on combatting *Rinkals* and in desperation used water and, if it was available, milk to wash out the eyes of the person sprayed. When alone in the bush some of the Pseudos told me that they cleaned the afflicted person's eyes with urine, using the urine of the first person able to produce it! Whether either of the treatments is recommended I know not to this day; but none of my men suffered any after-effects.

As mentioned previously, Larry Wateridge, a Tsetse Control Officer, had a research base in Tharaka where, amongst other things, he used to trap tsetse flies, paint them purple, and then release them. When they were next caught he would have some idea of their range and feeding habits (so I was told!). The tsetse used to feed heavily on the blood of baboons, monkeys and wild pigs, and Larry would set up traps to catch monkeys so that he could study how they coped with the parasite. As tsetse flies like shade, areas of bush were cut down to see if this would have the effect of banishing them from the district, which would enable the locals to think about bringing cattle into the area. We used to find monkey traps in the trees whilst on patrol, but never interfered with them. However, I gather that George and Joy Adamson would take down any traps they came across. Joy was the more aggressive in this respect.

A game scout from the Adamson camp came to me one day with a letter from George warning me that the lioness 'Elsa' had been released back into the wild and that as part of the rehabilitation the lioness was being encouraged to hunt for herself. This was a weaning process, he went on, and it should be remembered that Elsa was still partly tame; and whereas she might be attracted by humans, she was unlikely to prove dangerous. George went on to say that if we went shooting game, we should not be surprised if Elsa should hear the shots and come bounding along, and perhaps leap into the back of the truck. This would be normal behaviour. Elsa might also stroll into a tent; if this should happen it was better to stand still and let the beast sniff you, rather than make any sudden movement.

As one can imagine, George's letter sent the mind into overdrive. If a lioness came into the tent or truck, how did you recognise her as Elsa? Supposing she brought some of her 'wild' mates with her? What if the beast lay down in the tent for a nap? It was not the sort of problem to think about late at night. As it so happened, we saw nothing of the beast. But I did meet a lone, wandering geologist who was wandering along the banks of the Ura River with a geiger counter round his neck. Over a mug of *chai*, he told me that late one afternoon a lioness had poked her head into his tent, and that in panic he had shouted, 'Go away!' It did. On reflection he thought it must have been Elsa...

One of the local Tharakans who assisted us for some time, incurring in the process the wrath of some of Achole's gang, who caught him alone one day and roughed him up, was called Muatamuata. A thin and gangly man with a pronounced lisp, he caused amusement amongst the Pseudos when he called me 'machungwa' (oranges) rather than 'Mzungu' (European).

In February 1959, we had one of those unusual diversions that made life just that little bit different and interesting. This was the visit to Kenya of Queen Elizabeth the Queen Mother and, in particular, her visit to the Aberdare National Park.

Her Majesty was to picnic alongside a waterfall on a tributary of the Chania River which crosses the high moorlands of the mountains a good 9,000 feet above sea-level and is surrounded by thick forest which still then harboured a few die-hard Mau Mau. Under the overall supervision of Ian Henderson, on-the-ground security was to be provided by Blue Doctor Pseudos, some thirty in number, commanded by myself with mobile assistance from Mac (Dick MacLachlan) who would be with the Royal Party. We would form a screen in the bush (keep out of sight or you might scare the royal party). An outer screen covering the Treetops salient was to be provided by another Special Force Team commanded by Captain Bob Folliott, MC.

Once I had set the security screen in motion, I had to flee the bush and come into the picnic site, for part of my brief included keeping an eye on the picnic to be consumed by the Royal Party and, indeed, to taste a random selection of culinary items in the role of the 'Royal Taster'. All the wines, champagne and beer were lowered into the waterfall where they were kept ice-cold; as these items were sealed I reluctantly had to accept that they were most likely to be safe. I did test various 'open' samples of food, including sandwiches and the most delicious brandy-snaps. All went well. The men were in concealment and I was confident that nobody, not even an investigative journalist, could penetrate the *cordon sanitaire*.

Suddenly the 'five minute car' came over the brow of the moorland track. My instructions were to mobilise everyone once the early warning vehicle driven by Ian came into sight, and this I did.

The picnic for the Royal Party was provided by the Outspan Hotel (the former home of Baden Powell, the Chief Scout) and the hotel, along with some staff from the White Rhino Hotel, also in Nyeri, also provided the catering staff. As I shouted out that the Royal Party were just five minutes away, several nubile young ladies in various states of undress poured out of the picnic tents, provided by Kerr and Downey, on to the prickly heather of the moorlands in great panic. The problem was that Ian had decided to make a recce, ahead of his five-minute schedule, and in the process spread panic amongst the catering staff. With some embarrassment, I had to approach Esme Sparling, whom I knew from the White Rhino Hotel (where incidentally I first met Jim Corbett of 'Man Eater of Kumaon' fame) and explain to her that it was all a mistake.

I am not sure to this day whether in fact Ian, whose official Kikuyu name was *'Kinyanjui'*, but he had another colloquial name that escapes me now but had something to do with a smooth, bald, egg-like head, ever knew what panic he caused on the Aberdares.

When on Pseudo operations in the Aberdares, we frequently camped near the Chania and for obvious reasons nicknamed the area 'Frost Camp' it was always chilly and the young ladies in their underwear would confirm this.

The previous evening, on 15th February, I had escorted Mr Winter, whom I think had the Ford agency in Nyeri, on to the moorlands to catch some trout for the Royal breakfast. He was an artist at fishing and it was a delight, and very instructive, to watch him entice the trout from the tarn with the slight flick of his wrist, which put my cruder efforts, when fishing for the pot on patrol, to shame.

When the picnic was over and the Royal Party had departed for 'Treetops', it fell upon me to gather together all the expendable items, i.e. the latrines, wash-basins etc., but not the tents; then to burn or otherwise destroy them, and submit a certificate (good old Civil Service!) to this effect. This was necessary because on a previous Royal visit somebody had 'rescued' a loo seat, painted something like 'Guess who sat on here' and had then paraded at a party with the object round his neck. I was also aware, for I had served at the Royal Lodge at Sagana (which is now the President's Lodge) at the time an operational post, when I was permitted to live in the Equerry's quarters, that a visitor had one day had his photograph taken in the Royal bath! So it seemed sensible to prevent any such embarrassment by having the camping items destroyed, and I did.

On safari it was not uncommon to be sharing camp with just a couple of drivers as the only companions for several days on end. We brewed tea for each other and the standards of discipline were relaxed accordingly. There were two regular drivers. Kiprotich was a large Nandi with no finesse whose only requirements were women and booze, the cheaper the better. At the time when the frequency of atomic tests was making news headlines, Kiprotich equated having sex with Nairobi's ladies of leisure as being 'atomic'.

The other regular driver was Kinyola (Mwana Kinyungu – son of Kinyungu), a good-looking and mentally alert Mkamba, who was a good mimic and possessed of a captivating sense of humour. When sharing a mug of tea around the camp-fire of an evening, Kinyola would give recognisable imitations of his seniors, accurately portraying their mannerisms and gait. By all accounts his skit on me was a hoot but his embarrassment prevented him giving me a first-hand display. He also had a temper, and one day when I was drawing water from a stream, he fired a burst from his sub-machine-gun, allegedly over the heads of some Samburu tribesmen who had the nerve to water their cattle just upstream from our camp-site and, in the process foul our water supply. I had to severely admonish Kinyola for the unnecessary use of a firearm (and some of the bullets had splattered the water near me) and to reassure the peaceful Samburu that they had the right to water their cattle in the traditional way.

I must have mentioned to Ian Henderson several times that, with the Emergency coming to a close, I might well be looking for another job that would keep me close to the type of life that I had grown to love. Ian wrote to me to say that he had mentioned my name to Mervyn Cowie, Director of the National Parks, as a possible replacement for 'Tabs' Taberer in Tsavo. I spoke to Mervyn Cowie at the time of the Queen Mother's visit to the Aberdares. There had been a minor landslide on the track coming up from the Rift Valley and we were inspecting the damage. There were of course many other people after the National Parks job, some of them with impressive track records with game, so I decided not to apply.

The second introduction was to Sherbrooke Walker of 'Treetops'. He was planning another lodge on the Aberdares, and he required a manager with knowledge of game and the area. Ian had put my name forward adding that I also had knowledge of Mau Mau lore, that could conceivably interest the tourists. Whilst I had met members of Sherbrooke Walker's family, I had never met him. I was introduced at the Outspan Hotel, by Ian, where there was a short, very short interview.

'Do you have a second occupation, ladies' hairdresser or similar?'

'No,' said I and immediately lost interest. As did Sherbrooke Walker, who walked away to talk to another minion.

Kenya had its share of characters and it is nostalgic to recall contact with a few of them. The owner of the Silverbeck Hotel in Nanyuki, long since burnt down, was a Commander Logan Hook, a relative of the farmer-cum-hunter Raymond Hook. The Silverbeck Hotel stood astride the equator and there was an equatorial line marked across the bar, so that one could drink north or south of the line. I was sitting in the bar having a cool beer one morning, when Logan approached me and asked if I would like to join the 'Legion of Frontiersmen', which at that time was a largely symbolic organisation; though it had in the past served as a source of voluntary Commandos, as all recruits had to be competent riders and riflemen. As I prevaricated, for I prefer 'Shank's pony', Logan went on to ask what I thought of his proposal to invite 'Monty' to join. My lack of understanding led me to think that he was referring to Monty Moore, VC, a former Chief Game Warden of Tanganyika, who lived in retirement just below the Ndathi Police Post. Logan soon corrected me and made it clear that he was referring to the Field Marshal!

At Ndaragwa there were a collection of retired officials and others, of both sexes, who had large houses set along the top of a ridge known politely as 'Blood-Pressure Ridge' or, more commonly, 'Buggery Ridge'. There was an ex-District Commissioner called Sharpe who had a magnificent garden complete with several lakes. Sharpe was a leading member of the Kenya Horticultural Society. There was also Fabian Wallace, an ex-RAF pilot who had flown many VIPs, including Winston Churchill, who at that time was working as a KPR Superintendent in charge of the Central Province Operations Room at Nyeri. Fabian invited myself and several other young Police Inspectors to his house for the weekend, where we were well fed and watered (we drank beer whilst Fabian had brandy and milk, the latter at the request of his doctor). There were two or three other guests from the world of commerce in Nairobi, a couple of whom were a trifle effete. There being strength in numbers, the weekend passed virtually without incident. There was a book left casually on my bedside table explaining the raison d'être for homosexuality, and Fabian did poke his finger through my open-neck shirt, asking how far down the suntan went; but nothing else. We remained on friendly terms, separated by rank and sexuality only.

In the early days of the Emergency, the tactic adopted to combat Mau Mau gangs was a system of stop lines and sweeps. The call went out to police posts to provide 'one Inspector and eight men', the number that could be comfortably accommodated in the post's vehicle, to rendezvous at a given spot. A stop line would be set up and, from several miles away, a sweep in extended order would commence and come to a conclusion once everybody came up to the stop line. The number of those taking part would be re-enforced by the inclusion of KPR officers, farmers and even retired pensioners. One stalwart in Nanyuki, was colonel Rose Smith, a former Indian Army Officer who lived permanently in the Sportsman's Arms Hotel. The Colonel, who had in his day been something of a 'pig-sticker', would turn up for patrol in his khaki shorts and topee, armed with his own rifle. In 1954 the Colonel must have been in his late sixties.

The sweeps were seldom successful, and at best were a get-together of Inspectors and askaris from widely-spread posts, enabling them to swap news and experiences. Only once was I present when a gang was flushed due to a sweep operation. This took place in 1954 on Englebrect's farm on the Isiolo road, when all the gang escaped. One of the local experts on gang movements was Boyce Roberts, a local farmer who held the rank of District Officer. I seem to recall that he masterminded the Englebrect operation, and also many others in the area. Several times I was given a lift on the back of his Vincent 'Black Shadow', a 1000cc motor bike, as we checked the stop lines.

Although trackers were used from the earliest days of the Emergency (and in Nanyuki there was a very good Turkana called 'Moiya') the concept of 'Combat Tracker Teams' came much later; but when it came it proved to be far superior to the old ways and was a natural progression as past experiences were analysed and digested. There were several good tracker teams in the Central Province, and that of the former 'White Hunter' Peter Becker, which I later commanded, was a shining example. I was to meet Peter some twenty-five years later in Francistown, Botswana.

No one person can take the honours for the Pseudo gang technique. The idea was not new to Kenya, having been used in Malaya and Palestine, and probably elsewhere. In the Central Province we had the Special Force Camp at Kiganjo, where several Pseudo teams operated, usually with two expatriates to a team. I can recall that Noel Maynard operated with Bob Folliott and that one of their Pseudos was 'Chui' (leopard) whom I knew well. There were many others including Ian Pritchard, GM, and Eddie Brucelow, OBE.

These last two opened a watersports centre at Watamu, North of Mombasa, a place I visited on leave with Mike Hudson. It was a sad day when Ian hurt his back and was paralysed whilst water-skiing. He died several years later. It is possible that Eddie took his own life shortly afterwards.

SIX

THE ETHIOPIAN FRONTIER AND ELSEWHERE IN THE NORTHERN FRONTIER PROVINCE

The years 1960 to 1961 saw me astride the Ethiopian border, posted to Moyale where I succeeded the South African Brian Black as District Special Branch Officer. There are two Moyales: the Ethiopian side, usually spelt Moiyale, and consisting of a large collection of brothels, drinking dens and some trading stores; whereas the Kenya side was by far the more civilised township, with a large collection of trading stores, adequate petrol supplies and a thriving multi-racial club.

The huge 30 and 40-ton lorries that braved the boulder-strewn road south from Addis Ababa and Nagalle had to cross the border into Kenya, to replenish their tanks for the return journey, on roads that were more easily identifiable on the map than on the ground. The delights of the Ethiopian brothels did not escape the attention of the Kenya Police askaris and other government servants who always found an excuse to shop the other side of the border, even though they would agree that the stores on the Ethiopian side were very inferior.

On pay-days outside the Kenya police station at Moyale, you could always count on the presence of 'Mama Kelele' (Madame Noisy), a large Amharic (literally the mountain people, and perhaps the aristocrats of Ethiopia) who was always immaculately dressed in her flowing white robes. Mama Kelele, who ran the biggest, and allegedly the best brothel in Moiyale, would come to collect her dues. I was also interested in her for, at that time, she was the contact point for Kenyan and other East African students who were making their way overland to Addis Ababa to start their unauthorised bid for education in the Eastern bloc. These students would in most cases be travelling without travel documents; neither would they have the permission of the relevant East African Government.

Another interesting character in Moiyale was the Ethiopian District Commissioner with the resounding name of Mackonnon Fanta! He too was an Amharic, and he ruled over his district like a feudal lord. There was widespread corruption through-out the whole of Borana Province, and I can remember occasions when the Ethiopian police would go and raid their own villages and steal stock as they had not been paid for several months. Mackonnon Fanta had seen service both in Haile Selassie's bodyguard and the Ethiopian contingent during the Korean war. He wore his medal ribbons with pride on formal occasions.

Mackonnon Fanta would, infrequently, visit us in Moyale where he would be entertained at the club by our District Commissioner, George Webb and the Police Assistant Super-intendent, Nigel Marsh, the latter being well-known for his boxing prowess.

One day Mackonnon issued a general invitation for us to visit him and join in the celebrations for the Emperor Haile Selassie's birthday. Inspector John Moore and myself, accom-panied by a new Inspector, Dick, duly attended what turned out to be a very unusual party in a large hall-like structure in Moiyale. There was a plentiful supply of Johnny Walker whisky and crates of 7-Up, and my protestations that I was not a whisky drinker were politely but firmly ignored. I did manage to dilute the spirit with the sweet tasting 7-Up; however, whisky was poured into my glass constantly.

We had all agreed beforehand that as I was drinking, one of the others would give the Kenyan toast to the Emperor's continued good health, since one, I suspect it was Dick, would remain on soft drinks. I recollect that John Moore and myself drank a lot of whisky that evening, interspersed with great piles of an Ethiopian bread that has the flavour and consistency of Dunlopillow rubber. The meat segments in the goat stew were a little tough but child's play compared to the raw side of beef that hung suspended from the roof, from which one was invited to cut a strip off, dip it into a small bowl of powerful chilli sauce and slip it down, as chewing was something else.

At last it came to the final speeches, and with a head now beginning to whirl from the whisky, I looked at my companions to see who was going to give the speech. They both shrugged their shoulders, so up I rose and rambled through a loyal address to the Emperor's long life and continued good health, wincing once or twice when I heard myself hastily correcting the reference to Abyssinia (a name whose meaning refers to slave people!) by quickly substituting Ethiopia. There were no more disasters that night, and one of my companions drove us all safely back across the border.

Moyale, along with Marsabit and Isiolo, was one of the bomas in the Frontier, where officers were allowed to be accompanied by their wives. (Not to be sexist here, for I do not know of any European female officer who served in the Frontier and could have therefore been accompanied by her husband!) Being several hundred feet above the desert plains that stretched out to the South, Moyale was a healthy posting and, perched on the brow of the verdant Karabamba Hills, there was sufficient rainfall to have the luxury of a vegetable garden, as well as visits from the normally shy greater kudu which silently appeared during daylight amongst one's green vegetables. Fence posts, erected to keep out game, miraculously sprouted shoots and took root, such was the fertility of the soil.

Life was idyllic for anyone who enjoyed the quietness and loneliness of living largely alone, though to be sure, we did usually get together a couple of evenings a week at the club; and at weekends, we would play tennis on the court, lovingly tended and maintained by us all with red earth from termite hills which was rolled down with a mixture of sump oil. We bachelors appreciated the culinary skills of the expatriate wives, and I recall in particular Nigel's wife, Mimi, who was also an expert hand on the tennis court.

Moyale had a resident Mounted Section of sturdy ponies and there was also a Camel Section (*'Rhakoub'*) at El Wak ('the wells of God') for anyone keen on mounted patrols. I preferred to walk though I did hire local Boran camels to carry the *mzigo* (luggage). On foot with a few askaris, never more than five in number, we would walk from Moyale on patrols of seven to ten days along the border area, both east and west. These are highly scenic places, in many parts extremely mountainous, where local people cared little for international boundaries; that is, until some government official tries to tax them. There was however the problem of obtaining water and on some safaris we had to nip over the Ethiopian border to replenish our large camel *barramills*, and get back smartly again before the locals warned the Ethiopian police that there was a Ferenji (foreigner) around. We referred to them as the 'dreaded Habash' and they would sometimes patrol parallel with us on their side of the border, waiting to see what we got up to.

Once when we were negotiating the border towards the Kenya Police Border Post at Gurar two days' walk from Moyale, we needed water. It was the usual situation of 'Ilhumdililie' (By the Grace of God) when water was used without thought for the morrow. The only water in the district was across the border at Gadaduma. We visited the wells at 2 a.m., hoping to find them quiet. The place was seething with Boran and I guess it always is. Quickly filling the twenty-gallon barramills with muddy water, we hastened back across the border, where we camped alongside the manyatta of Chief Gufu Sora of the Boran.

An hour or so later, three Ethiopian police officers, armed with short-barrel rifles, burst into the camp and joined us round the fire. After an exchange of greetings, they asked us what we were doing camped inside Ethiopia. We insisted we were well inside Kenya (now!). There followed a lengthy tirade from the three visitors telling us why our camp-site was definitely in Ethiopia. It was beginning to look like a minor border incident: we were unarmed, apart from a ·22 rifle to shoot birds for the pot, and the three Ethiopians were obviously narked, having failed to apprehend us poaching water.

Just when things were getting heated, in walked Chief Gufu Sora, a well-respected figure, who had heard the commotion and had come to investigate. We put the boundary question to the chief, who said that his manyatta was in Kenya, to whom he paid his poll tax, so that was that. It would appear that our visitors were trying it on but they could not browbeat the Chief of the Boran. Gufu Sora was a tall, white-bearded figure who always used a liberal application of talcum powder. Whilst drinking milk in his hut, I saw a tin of 'Bint El Sudan' on the bed and I believe that was his partiality.

After the Ethiopians had left as suddenly as they had arrived, we continued on our way south-east to the police post at Takaba, before heading west to Ajao Hill. At Ajao I remember watching the scrawny shoats coming in to water at a well set in the side of the hill near its peak, which was at over 3,000 feet. The shoats when they left were swollen with water and looked huge, and my askaris pointed out the dangers of buying a beast just after it had been watered! The well at Ajao bore the imprint of a British sapper's name and rank in the cement surround that had been helpfully added to the natural rock to prevent erosion.

Walking in this part of the district was relatively easy and there was little if any of the porous lava rock that one has to negotiate in the Dida Galgulu plain that we tackled later in the year. A lot of Boran and others came to greet us and seemed surprised to see a mzungu on foot, until it was explained to them that I was allergic to camels! Both men and women, of all ages, are apt to treat such visitors well and camel milk, usually in the congealed state that they favour, was always offered. The opportunity was also sought to wheel out all the sick and injured, and my specially prepared medicine chest was in great demand. My medical knowledge is non-existent, but aspirins and bandages were handed out and Jeyes fluid dispensed in small quantities for cleaning purposes. The recipients were always grateful even though we were offering them little more than comfort.

We did encounter a couple of really trying cases: two young herdboys had picked up a World War II grenade that had lain hidden on the ground since the hostilities there in the 1940s and, not knowing what the object was, they had hammered it with a rock until it blew up. Both had serious arm, body and head abrasions and, after cleaning them up, we put them on a

camel and sent them and their elders off to the police post at
Buna, with a note asking the Post Commander to put them on a
passing trader's vehicle to Moyale. When we arrived at Buna
the next day, this had been done and I think both lads survived
the ordeal. Walking in this part of the frontier, it was still
possible to come across the rusted wrecks of old army vehicles,
and pieces of what looked like early World War II planes.

From Buna we had an uphill walk back to Moyale via
Korondil Hill, a peak we scaled for the view across the baked
Korondere plain. Sitting on top of the hill, again a peak
something over 3,500 feet high, one was conscious of the warm
breeze wafting across one's face and the absolute silence as you
gazed out over hundreds of square miles of desert. The silence
was so complete, that it hurt my ears...

My fascination with the Ethiopian border was really part of my
Special Branch duties of keeping an eye on what we broadly
termed 'border affairs'. This description encompassed illegal
crossings, the activities of Ethiopian security forces, water and
border disputes and virtually any other act or incident, that
could have cross-border repercussions. Local politics was at a
low ebb and only got up a little steam when both British and
Italian Somalilands gained their independence in 1960 when a
few of the local Somali traders, who were in the minority,
started to talk of the 'Greater Somalia' concept. I can remember
George Webb, our District Commissioner, addressing a local
gathering of dignitaries at a 'Tea Party', held to commemorate
British Somaliland's independence. He startled the Somalis in
the audience by saying, in Kiswahili, that 'even the son of a
lunatic can get his freedom, but it really depends what he does
with it!'

One day whilst on safari west of Moyale, following the de
facto border, a series of cement pillars that had been set up by
the boundary commission, separating Kenya from Ethiopia, we
decided, for a little light relief to climb Forole Mountain that
rears to over 6,500 feet. The area appeared quiet and there were
no reports of any raiders from Ethiopia, so we climbed
unarmed and with a minimum of kit as it was very hot. We did
manage to reach the top after a long clamber, and Galgalo and

myself left our names in a small jar that contained a list left there by some visiting expatriate. On reaching the base of Forole, we were all gasping for a drink and as it was a few more hours' march to our camp we decided to scout around for some water. We found some damp spots in a wadi where elephants had been digging and, after scrapping a small hole in the gravel and inserting a mug, we were rewarded with a trickle of water after ten minutes or so. I was allowed to drink first and I did so before the gravel in the mug had settled, and was promptly sick!

After being picked up in our Austin lorry, a three-tonner with twin wheels at the rear, we set off back to Moyale. En route we were stopped on the dirt track by a huge herd of camels that rather surprisingly was being driven by a bevy of Boran maidens (the Somalis would have called them *gabdos*). They were very young, very nubile and their skins glistened with good health as they ran to and fro, naked to the waist and giggling as they made a hash of trying to control the camels. As we admired the maidens, Sub-Inspector Galgalo was getting impatient, since the lorry was still stationary. There was also no doubt that the maidens were 'selling their eyes' to one or two of the askaris. Galgalo shouted out something in Boran that absolutely convulsed the maidens but they did clear the road. When we were further down the track with the familiar curtain of desert dust raising in our wake, I asked Galgalo what he had said. A simple translation from the vernacular produced the line, 'Move, or I'll lay the lot of you!'

Roaming out from a camp early one evening, equipped with a short ·22 rifle to shoot a kanga (a guinea-fowl or vulturine), myself and a colleague were on foot in open thorn-bush country when we came across a full-grown lion with a huge mane some twenty yards from us. As hair stood on end, mine not the lion's, and the fear shot through my limbs, the lion dropped down from view, and I thought the beast was stalking us!

The lion reappeared a short distance away, nearer and looking right at us without making a noise. I could see the beast quivering and it flashed through my mind that it was about to charge so, with an instinctive swing, up came the rifle and I fired the ·22, aiming for the eyes and getting two shots off before the lion dropped down again. I had, I thought, another few rounds in the magazine and when the head of the lion showed itself again, I repeated the action being convinced by now that this was our only chance of escape. The lion did not show itself again, so both of us walked away slowly, backwards at first, until we were some distance away, when we high-tailed it back to camp and collected a vehicle.

On returning we found the lion almost dead and we put it out of its misery from a safe distance. We were then able to appreciate the full saga and realise that our escape had more to do with the lion than our own puny efforts. The lion stank to high heaven. It had one paw almost severed by a wire noose that was still in place and the wound had gone gangrenous. The lion was badly emaciated and had been on its last legs. The magnificence of the lion's mane had hid the plight of the beast from us, and we might well have been able to walk away from the initial scene without resorting to the risky use of a ·22. But I think, in the end, the conclusion reached was the best for the lion.

There was a footnote to this episode. George Webb included brief details of the incident in his monthly report. This was read by Leslie Pridgeon, the Provincial Police Commander, who then called upon me to submit a report explaining what I, an ex-officio Game Warden, was doing shooting big game with a weapon of far too small a calibre!

The Duty Police Inspector at Moyale also had to act as Immigration Officer, for there were none of that ilk in the Northern Frontier. Duly equipped with a couple of rubber stamps, and a rudimentary knowledge of the Immigration Act, one was let loose to disfigure foreign passports. There was a trickle of adventurous types, usually 'Germans from Hamburg' trekking through Africa, who came across the border from the wilds of Ethiopia with great-expectations. More often than not, they were seeking a pat on the back for having made it across the appallingly bad roads in Ethiopia, and they would then ask directions to the nearest hotel. To the more thick-skinned travellers, one would tell them with a straight face, 'keep going straight on for 450 miles, until you hit the tarmac.' But to those with problems, usually of a mechanical nature, or perhaps with a young family, we would try to be more understanding.

A Belgian family arrived one evening with three young children. They were en route overland back to the Congo, where the father worked for one of the large plantations. I felt sorry for them and took them into my house where they were fed and had hot baths, the cook working overtime to stoke up the Kuni (wood) fire under the old oil drums that was my hot water system. The family were provided with camp-beds and they stayed the night. The husband thanked me the next morning, as the family left for Wajir and Isiolo, adding that he did not know how I could live under such primitive conditions. Apparently in the Congo the family had a large colonial bungalow with air conditioning and all mod cons.

I never heard from them again, not so much as a postcard. I do hope they survived the bloodbath that followed in the Belgium Congo, for they were a nice couple with delightful children. It was pointless to tell them that in Moyale we considered our housing and lifestyle to be good by Northern Frontier standards!

Moyale was a multi-racial boma, and this was reflected in our club with European, Asian and Muslim members. Our doctor was Dr Ventecatcha, a Hindu and conjurer-up of exotic curries which was always followed by tinned peaches and tinned cream. Dr Ventecatcha would horrify the more squeamish of his lunch guests when he related in some detail his physical efforts in trying to pull the remnants of a two-foot tape worm from a young Boran youth. It was better to sit at the furthest end of the lunch table as the horrified faces of his guests seem to urge the Doctor on to even more gory tales.

There were Goan officers in the Administration and these, along with several Arabs and Somalis from the trading sector, formed a local football team. Usually I was the only European. We played 'internationals' against the Ethiopians, on both sides of the border. One of the stalwarts, the son of a one-armed Arab Trader named Bumrugga (cruelly known as 'Rumbugger'),

was an intelligent and articulate young man with whom we
had many a laugh, particularly when we played in Ethiopia
and came back with Italian pasta and chianti. One day I did talk
Eddie Edwards, one of our stalwart Kenya Police Airwing
pilots who kept us in touch with civilisation, into having a
game. It was indeed unfortunate that poor Eddie ricked his
ankle and flew back to Nairobi in some discomfort.

Moving down to the hot, arid plains of Wajir in May 1961,
where a few months later I also took the Special Branch in
Mandera under my wing, was a great contrast. Wajir is a
trading centre that owes its livelihood to its deep wells that
always seem to hold water even in times of drought. Day and
night there is a constant stream of stock, mainly camels, that
come in to water. Being a trading centre with numerous stores –
Somali, Arab and Pakistan – and also a livestock sales centre, it
was host to a never-ending passage of Somali tribesmen from
numerous clans. As they are born masters of intrigue, and
everyone a budding politician, the Special Branch presence was
there to monitor political and tribal aspirations, so that the
powers in Nairobi could be kept in the picture.

Living accommodation in Wajir for government servants
was very much along the lines of 'Beau Geste'. The houses were
huge white painted structures, constructed of a mixture of
cement and hardened mud. Most were double-storey, complete with upper battlements. The flat roof contained an area
known as the 'cage'. This was a simple structure of four pillars
that held up a modest roof, to protect one from the occasional
shower, but all sides were opened to the elements. Due to the
heat, most people slept in the cage which was reached directly
from ground level by a concrete staircase.

Owing to the temperatures in the *jilaal* (hot summer period),
it was wise to keep even items such as potatoes in the modest
coolness provided by the charcoal or paraffin fridge. The great
cure for a malfunctioning paraffin fridge was to load it into the
back of a truck and drive over some bumpy roads, which
apparently bucks up the acetylene gas!

Wajir is situated on solid rock, the wells having been bored
almost vertically down some 60 to 80 feet. Drinking water was

gathered from the modest rains by down-pipes into a large galvanised tank. Mine was of a 100 gallon capacity, but seldom if ever full. Due to it being a most precious commodity, all taps to the fresh-water tank had small padlocks, and the contents zealously guarded. Peering down from above into the tank was not to be recommended for the faint-hearted, for on the bottom of the tank could be seen numerous skeletons of over-anxious geckos that had ventured once too far!

Water for washing and cleaning was provided by a small team of prisoners from the local jail. They were low-category, crime-wise prisoners who wheeled small drums around on a trolley and doled one out a very modest ration. It was wise not to drink this water, for it contains minor particles of mica that can cause havoc with the urinary organs, and is said to give one the feeling of 'peeing razor blades'. There was also a Health Department analysis of the well water at Wajir that stated that the water was heavily contaminated with camel urine which had permeated down through the rock over the years that the camels had been watered there! Making tea with the well water was drinkable as long as milk was not added. To put the milk in would turn the concoction into a total disaster, for it would remain black in colour however much milk one added.

The rock strata also made it impossible to sink 'long-drops' for lavatories, so the bucket system was in force. The 'night soil' was removed early in the morning by a team of prisoners. As the Kiswahili for lavatory is *Choo*, the removal teams were known as the 'abominable choo men'. It could be quite disconcerting to be seated on the choo early in the morning and to suddenly hear the bucket being whipped away from under you and then replaced with a loud clatter. It was not always possible to hear the donkey-cart approaching, as my house was alongside the wells and there was the constant noise, both by day and night, of the camel bells sounding as the beasts were watered.

One of the local characters was chief Abdi Ogli of the Mohammed Zubier of the Ogaden. A short Somali with a husky voice, he always dressed in pure white robes and he loved to talk but would seldom give any indication of what the

Mohammed Zubier were up to, although he loved to run down the Aulihan, whom he likened to *michwa* (white ants or termites) as they 'gnaw away out of sight!' Chief Abdi Ogle was keen to pass on the news that he worked for 'British Intelligence' during the Second World War; in fact I believe that he acted as a scout for the Army during the campaign in the Northern Frontier Districts against the Italian Forces.

Inter-tribal disputes, usually centred around water and grazing rights, was the daily bread and butter, and there were only minor rumblings of the displeasure that the Somalis would later on express more forcibly at the then still distant prospect of 'African Rule'.

The watering of stock, particularly camels, was an enthralling sight: the Somali herdsman would hurl his giraffe-skin bucket down into the depths of the well; there would be a distant thud as the bucket hit the waters; then he would haul in the rope and pour the water into a small trough, out of which the camel would drink with a surprisingly delicate action for such a bad-tempered beast.

Elsewhere in the Wajir district, there were other wells of a less vertical nature than those at either El Wak or Wajir centre. One went down, zig-zagged into the depths as access was gained by natural faults in the rock. It took some eight men to ferry the water from the bottom to the top, and each man could only just see the man either side of him, the others being out of sight. The bottom man would thump the skin bucket on the water, which set the rhythm for his chanting colleagues above. The sound was primitive and hypnotic and it echoed throughout the 30-odd foot caverns. It was hot down there and now and again one of the Somalis would empty the contents of the bucket over himself to cool down.

Maribou storks gathered in great profusion around any form of habitation, as they are great carrion feeders. They always look to me like undertakers, as they strut along on their spindly legs with their black wings giving the impression of having their hands clasped behind their backs. As the maribous climbed high on the thermals, there was occasionally a loud bang as a bone descended from a great height and crashed onto the roof of the 'cage', where someone might be having a siesta during the heat of the afternoon. Various bones were collected and compared. It was very unnerving to discover that the bones were human . . . it was even possible to identify an arm or a leg.

As the result of enquiries, as they say, it was soon established that the Provincial Medical Officer, a delightful Irishman by the name of Jimmy Clearkin, who carried out his weekly surgeries on a Tuesday, handed over the discarded limbs to his Somali staff for burial. The problem was that the burials were too shallow and the cunning old maribou had learnt how to get a free lunch!

Being an inquisitive bird, the maribous used to perch on the top of of the vertical wells in Wajir and gaze lovingly at their reflections in the water some 80 feet down. On some occasions the birds became so besotted that they would tumble down to the depths below, where they would thrash around in panic. Lowering a bucket and trying to hook the bird out proved hopeless, and any human going down on a rope would be well and truly skewered by the bird's long beak, which could wreak havoc in such a confined space. To leave the bird in the well would only add to the potency of the water, so the only alternative was to shoot them and then fish them up un-opposed.

Outside the residence of the District Commissioner, the lean and amiable Peter Fullerton, there were a series of shallow ponds which were filled daily with well water by the prisoners for the benefit of the local birdlife. During the morning this mainly consisted of doves, pigeons and starlings; but of an afternoon, countless thousands of sand-grouse would whirl in to water. On some occasions they would darken the sky with their numbers as they would gyrate down in perfect formation, fuss around the water, drink and then dampen their breast feathers to ferry water to their chicks. Whilst all would gaze in awe at this magnificent sight, the treacherous Marabou would wander up and down, pretending to look the other way and then suddenly gulp down a dove in one snap and then look suitably surprised when the other birds sidled away from its presence. The sand-grouse would continue to fly in beautiful formations, their whirring wings and precision flying being a wonder to see. The birds seemed to move as one and there was no untidiness in the patterns of their flight.

Stricken down with some ailment that resisted any accurate diagnosis, I bared myself in front of Jimmy Clearkin for a thorough medical check-up. Jimmy could not find anything amiss but as I was seeing double on occasions and also hallucinating, he referred me to Nairobi, with a sealed letter for the doctor. I took off in a Kenya Police Cessna for Nairobi, somewhat troubled by Jimmy's report (I had opened and read the letter) that I might be suffering from 'organic decay'. In due course I was admitted to the Queen Elizabeth Hospital and allocated a bed. After disrobing and getting into bed, I noticed one of the Staff Nurses removing my clothes from the small cupboard and taking them away. I queried why my clothes were being removed and the Staff Nurse replied, 'We know about you chaps from the Frontier!'

A few days later I was able to solve the mystery. It would seem that a couple of months previously, a District Officer from Wajir, one Robin Dalgleish, famed for his wearing of a sealskin waistcoat in the heat of the NFD, having been admitted to the 'Queen Elizabeth', was found by Matron, on her midnight rounds, dressed in his dinner jacket. The Matron, after some moments of shocked silence, said that she hoped Dalgleish did not think he was going into town. 'No,' said he, 'I have just come back.'

Hence the removal of my scanty NFD kit!

My stay in hospital, although brief for they could find nowt wrong with me, lasted one week. Both doctor and nurse took great delight in explaining in detail that I was to be given a 'lumbar punch'. They told me that if the needle should inadvertently hit my spine, I would know all about it, and that I would probably leap right off the couch. Adopting the feotal position, with a mark drawn towards the base of my spine where the needle was to be inserted, I lay unmoving until the nurse told me that the doctor was about to insert the needle. I must have shuddered. The nurse leaned over me again and told me there was nothing to worry about. I could not tell her that it was the whisky on her breath that made me shudder! I was to meet the doctor later on at Lanet when he was issuing death certificates and administering to the wounded after the mutiny in the Kenya Army had been put down.

My sole remaining escapade whilst in hospital was to convey to an Italian lorry driver from Addis Ababa, in Kiswahili, for he could not speak English, that the trainee nurse was going to administer a suppository. Along with a fellow conspirator, we examined the Swahili possibilities ranging from *kifuniko* (a cork) to a *risasi* (a bullet), settling, I am ashamed to admit, for the latter. His face told it all!

For relaxation in Wajir, we had the Royal Wajir Yacht Club. Of similar construction to our houses, it was a single-storey mud and cement building with a *makuti* (palm frond) roof. Shaped in the form of a ship, our place of relaxation contained a small bar and a few chairs and tables, where the male community would meet of an evening and at weekends. On a few rare occasions, we would entertain various white ladies that were passing through with official approval. The club had a self-made coat of arms, a splendid club tie – a camel surmounted by a crown – and honorary titles for the handful of members, the 'Commodore' being the District Commissioner and so on. My house was right next door to the club, in African terms, and I was the Chaplain! The club had a verandah in the form of a ship's bow, with a small retaining wall giving the impression of bulwarks: all very outlandish and exactly what visitors expected in the very different atmosphere that prevailed in the frontier. There was an ancient visitors' book that bore an entry circa 1920s, of a visiting lady who recorded her occupation as 'Nun' but whose contribution under the remarks column cast considerable doubt on the veracity of her vocation. It would seem that those who passed before us were equally as light-hearted and free-thinkers like ourselves.

There was also a largely unsuccessful tennis court, the correct proportions of termite soil and sump oil, seeming to evade us. A humble 'swimming pool', little more than an emergency water-tank, never achieved popularity as the well water gave nasty ear infections to those who were beguiled by its sparkling reflections.

There were other interesting residents in the bachelor boma of Wajir. Colin Watkins, a bespectacled young man with an active sense of humour who, whilst I was awaiting a picnic lunch with my other colleagues, deposited a green jelly on my head! Colin went on to have a distinguished career in the Royal Military Police, retiring with the rank of Lieutenant-Colonel.

There was also our transport officer, John Norris, known as 'Look Here', his favourite form of address. I had first met John at Sagana Police Post in the days when the road there was a bright-red *murram* affair. In those days John was restoring a 12-cylinder Bugatti, a massive beast known to the locals as the kifaru (rhino) due to the machine's massive size and tendency to issue hearty snorts. The beast used to hurtle up the dirt road at 90 mph, with the occupants wearing goggles, as failure to do so could result in a black eye from a wandering borer beetle – some of whom measured an inch or so across. John, a lifetime bachelor, although he did adore the ladies, used to amuse (and impress) us with tales of his younger years. Apparently his father gave him a dress allowance that John used to spend on spares for his Bentley which he raced at Brooklands.

In the District Administration, Peter Fullerton's number two was Henry Wright, a stocky and athletic individual who joined the dubas (tribal police) in some cross-country running. One day Mike Baldwin, one of the travelling armourers, flew into Wajir with a few nurses to attend a party. Henry succumbed to the charms of one Maureen and we saw less of him from that day on. Henry and Maureen went on to 'squash grapes' in Australia.

Our Medical Officer, Jimmy, was an avid customer of the Wajir club. Outwardly a quiet and inoffensive man, he was however possessed of a wicked sense of humour. Sitting in the corner of the bar and only to ready to speak to visitors, he would rise politely from his seat, order them a cold beer and extend his hand in friendship. As he shook hands, Jimmy would let loose a giant hunting spider (some of which had a six-inch span or more) out of his palm where the insect had been confined, and roll up with laughter as the spider scuttled up the arm of the visitor who by this time was almost apoplectic! Jimmy caught me once, so I knew exactly how the victims felt.

Further light relief was provided by the arrival of an all-female safari group riding camels and led by John Alexander, a former National Parks Warden, whom I had glimpsed once or twice from the bamboo of the Aberdares a few years previously. The safari group were allowed to stay for the night and we entertained them in the Royal Wajir that evening. There were only a few of us in the boma, but we did our best to look after our visitors who were inquisitive as to our lifestyles and how exactly we coped living in the arid wastes. Our visitors were delightful ladies, well-educated, well-heeled and undoubtedly of good breeding. It would be true to say that compliments were exchanged both ways. As the night wore on and the ladies were contemplating another day in a camel saddle the following morning, we departed to bed.

Next morning I awoke in my 'tower' (some called it 'tower', others 'cage') just after dawn, and in the half-light I was frantically scrambling around for my underpants and shorts. They had vanished! I was beginning to wonder whether a hungry hyena had braved my stairs and removed the 'man smelling' items, as they have a tendency to do in times of drought, when glancing up to the near horizon I caught sight of an unusual 'signal' flying from the District Commissioner's 'yardarm'. There, fluttering in the early morning breeze, was a collection of male underwear and shorts, mine included, that had been gathered up in the night hours by our industrious visitors, completely undetected. What a laugh, and full marks to the ladies for a successful operation!

Some of my colleagues had also lost their clothing and we were calling to each other from our flat roofs, exchanging information and waving enthusiastically at the swaying camels as the culprits filed out of Wajir, on their way north. The lady that I remember well from this episode was named Pamela. Dark-haired and attractive with eyes that glistened with humour, she was in fact Lady Pamela Egremont, the wife of Lord Egremont, Private Secretary to Harold Macmillan, both prior to and after he became Prime Minister.

In daily lives that contained little of the routine, some semblance of order was set by two regular monthly meetings held with my uniformed colleagues and officers from the Administration: these were the District Intelligence Committee, which dealt with political and tribal matters; and the District Security Committee, which concentrated on the security of airstrips and other key installations. As Mandera was also under my wing, these meetings were duplicated in that boma, too.

As the minutes of both meetings were circulated directly to various government and military addresses in Nairobi, it became something of a problem to find anything of real substance to record at the Security meetings. It is true we had an airstrip but the only structure was a windsock flying from a discarded section of water-pipe. There were no water, electricity or sewage plants to defend. We made mention from time to time of an emergency supply of barbed wire, to fence the airstrip off in times of trouble, but the wire could not always be located, as the desert scrub covered the coils. Our emergency holding centre for prisoners, should tribal warfare or insurrection come about, was always useful as a long stop. This was a high-walled, roofless structure, entrance to which was gained by a long wooden ladder (for there were no doors) which would then be removed. The fact that the walls had a black stripe running round the interior, and a court marked out on the floor, did not help disguise the fact that the holding centre looked remarkably like a squash court.

Was the 'Holding Centre' ever used? Yes, when I climbed on to the top of the back wall one day and took a cine film of Peter Fullerton playing squash with Colin Watkins, a Kenya Police Inspector, both of whom were deft hands with a squash racket.

After the monthly round of meetings in Mandera, sometime in mid-1961, I was enjoying my sandwich and a cold beer alongside the small pool at the Mandera Club in company, I believe, with Inspector John Fyfe. There were just the two of us plus the District Commissioner, amongst the expatriates in the boma, when an RAF Argosy transport plane commenced circling alarmingly low overhead. The lumbering plane got lower and lower until suddenly a hatch opened on the top of the fuselage, a figure appeared and a Verey light was fired! The plane then turned towards the dirt airstrip where it landed a few minutes later amidst giant clouds of dust. As it was normal practice to go and meet any plane that circled a boma and then landed, off we sped in a Land Rover, urged on by the added excitement of the huge size of the plane and the mystery, to us, of the Verey light.

Various doors on the Argosy opened, and out poured several Land Rovers, trailers, guns and a lot of troops. The plane, en route from Nairobi to Aden, had developed engine trouble and, as Mandera was marked on their maps as an emergency strip, down they came. The net result was that a boma that had a maximum of a handful of expatriates was now swollen to well over forty. We looked after the crew and soldiers as best we could. The next morning we were host to another Argosy that flew in with a repair team. Eventually, both planes left us, having provided much excitement, clouds of dust and a severe reduction in the stocks of Tusker beer.

Being on safari in the NFD, in the largely dry climate that prevailed for most of the year, was to me majestic. Striding out behind the pack camels without a care in the world and governed only by the desire to put twenty or so miles in before the heat of the day arrived, meant an early start but the chilliness of dawn had its own beauty and, hopefully, by 2 p.m. the camels could be couched and camp set up. Meeting up with other camel trains was always an event and it was pleasing to note that, on most occasions, news was freely exchanged and, if needed, assistance given with water or medical supplies. The latter was usually our privilege.

Sometimes in the heat it was difficult to make out at a distance what sort of camel train was approaching. The heat mirage made identification difficult and on occasions the shimmering figures turned out to be ostriches or gazelles.

Approaching a well depression one day, we encountered a large train of heavily-laden Boran camels, one of whose number refused to go any further. It received numerous beatings administered with both sticks and hide whips but would not rise to its feet. The beast squatted down with its swaying load and I believe would have died on the spot, rather than get up and journey on. The Boran had a cure. They lit a small fire under the creature's hind quarters and when its skin began to scorch, it lurched to its feet with a mighty roar and joined the other camels, apparently none the worse for wear!

Tribesmen were, generally speaking, kind to their animals and had great affection for their camels and cattle whom they treated as individuals. Some of their methods of treating sick camels might raise a few eyebrows amongst Europeans; but in an area where there were no practising civilian veterinary staff, they had to make do with established tribal cures and treatments. I came upon some Somali members of the Herti–Dolbahanta tribe one day and watched them as they administered to a sickly camel. The beast had been clawed by a lion and the Somalis first of all cauterised the wounds by laying on hot knives from a blazing fire, then they extracted the thin black tube from a torch battery (containing carbon?), crushed the tube into powder and then pushed the powder, none too gently, into the camel's wounds. The beast roared a couple of times, then got to its feet and trundled off.

There were times when the grunting of lions made it difficult to sleep. This was particularly so around the Sololo area where we had set up camp for the night at the foot of Borole, a mountain that peaked at 4,500 feet. Whether it was one lion or a pride we never found out but the grunts and roars echoed round the surrounding hills all night. I asked Chief Gufu Sora of the Boran what I was to make of the odd saucer of milk that was sometimes found at the base of a hill or mountain. He smiled as he replied that some of his people still followed their old ways and, unlike him, were still pagans. I gently probed further by asking what the old ways were. 'They worship the big snake,' he said, a reference to the African rock python!

Along the Ethiopian border the Marie Theresa 'Thaler', a large silver coin minted, I think, in Austria was in common usage. All the copies that I have seen, including those in my possession, bear the date 1780. According to the Ethiopians, the coin is popular in their country as Theresa is a large-breasted woman. The coin is certainly popular and no doubt the silver content also had something to do with its popularity.

The Kenya Police Airwing, particularly during the rainy season, was a vital link with civilisation. Post really would arrive by 'airmail' and not the haphazard trader's lorries that would be subject to breakdowns and other delays. The Airwing were a boon if one was going on leave for it was possible to be in Nairobi in three to four hours, including stops en route; whereas by road it could take a day or a day and a half. I am reminded of John Moore, who occupied the house next to mine in Moyale: he went on one week's leave but became bogged down in the rains en route to Isiolo, having to swim across Lagh Bogal with his suitcase floating on a do-it-yourself raft, constructed out of planks and a couple of oil drums. It took John nine days to reach Isiolo, where he was gratified to have it confirmed that one's leave in the Frontier did not start until you left the Province!

A fellow passenger in an Airwing Cessna one day was an Anglican bishop, flying in to test candidates in the Boran language. As we were flying over the wastes of the frontier, part of his parish, and I could see the pilot's chart had stamped across it the inscription 'this area is unsuitable for flying over in one-engined aeroplanes', I thought to keep my mind off our single whirring propeller by asking the Bishop how many converts he had in the Frontier.

He replied, 'One to be certain and possibly one other.' What an honest man.

One senior administration officer in the Frontier once showed me a letter from the Provincial Commissioner marked 'highly confidential', which concerned the alleged over-fraternisation of some administrative officers with Somali maidens. What did I think about the subject? Was such a matter reported on by Special Branch? I had come across several progeny of former administration officers in the Moyale district. They were half-Boran, with handsome features, who received some sort of maintenance payments from their expatriate fathers, paid via the local post office. But I made it clear that we were not in the busybody business; that there was far too much sniping by some administration officers, and it was not my intention to join them ... so it's safe with me!

At about the same time, as I was preparing to go on safari with an administration officer, he pulled some underclothes out of his drawer to take with him and several classified documents fell out with his pants. He blushed as he hastily apologised for not having returned the papers to his office safe. I assured the officer that we all made mistakes.

I only met one administration officer on a foot-cum-camel patrol and that was Robin Dalgleish from Wajir. Most others that I came across had the full range of tents, chairs and baths. Robin used to share meals with his dubas, though this of course was in the days when they could be trusted. Later some of them were to prove most treacherous to their officers.

Every year in the Northern Frontier, the Kenya Meat Commission (KMC) held livestock auctions at the main trading centres in the Frontier, where they bought stock from the local Boran, Somalis and other tribes. It was commonplace to see George Low and his wife set up camp alongside a cattle boma. They would have a small tent, which always contained a large double bed, and a camp-table and chairs. George, with his Somali neopara (headman), would handle the buying side, whilst his wife kept the ledger and paid out cash to the sellers. It was interesting to watch the turbanned neopara at work. He would go off and chat with individual sellers in the shade of a thorn-tree, listen to the price they had in mind and then go back to George and report. Listening in, I was able to conclude that the final agreed price was invariably a good 10% less than the seller had floated.

These auctions were fascinating, bringing in tribesmen from all over the district, and proved to be a good time for picking up tribal moods and concerns. The buyers' contact with the outside world, fresh supplies of food, more cash and always a plentiful supply of ice in a large thermos, was maintained by single-engine Cessnas that flew in and out of the various bush air-strips. Once the cattle were purchased, they were driven at leisure by KMC personnel – later to become the African Livestock Organisation (ALMO) – down-country to Nanyuki where they were fatted, usually on white-owned farms, before their dispatch to Athi River for slaughter.

With the advent of the *Shifta* problem, the movement of large herds of cattle had to be carefully planned otherwise they could easily be hijacked and sold over the border in Somalia. There were some 6,000 head of cattle to be moved, some from as far distant as Moyale on the Ethiopian border. Due to the sheer volume of stock and the sparse water supplies en route, Hector Douglas, of the Kenya Veterinary Department, ruled that the herds should be split up into groups of approximately 1,500, which made them more manageable and gave the Kenya Army pumping teams time to draw up water for each successive herd. Escorts were provided by the Kenya Army and the Kenya Police, the latter being inclusive of several GSU platoons.

My part in the so-called 'Operation Cowboy', as Officer Commanding Isiolo Division, was to supervise, along with Major Maingi of the Kenya Army, the herds' progress through our district. There were no major problems and certainly no loss of stock to the *Shifta*. On one sortie from Isiolo, we did encounter a large herd of Samburu cattle, grazing illegally in the Somali Leasehold Area. The *Morani*, all armed with spears, took off on sighting us. We seized a token number of cattle, placed them under guard for escort back to Isiolo, where they would be held pending a court case, and went to proceed on our way.

As I turned my back on the Samburu Moran, whom I had been informing about the course of action we were taking, a couple of them made a typical spear thrower's crouching run, which resulted in my sergeant firing a burst from this SMG over their heads and, fortunately to one side of me. No one was hit and the Morani took the hint and sullenly withdrew.

Isiolo is largely populated by members of the Herti–Issack Somali tribe. They live in a number of small villages with the prefix 'Kampi' which probably points towards their ancestors being former members of the Kenya African Rifles (KAR) who were granted land tenure in reward for service during the First World War.

As Divisional Commander, my opportunities to go on operational patrols were limited. Isiolo was a Provincial HQ, and it is a well-known fact that living on their doorstep, so as to speak, one was much more likely to get the casual HQ officer visiting, particularly when there was work to be done. Nevertheless, I did manage to get a night patrol in with Ken Smith, Game Warden, and his Somali Scouts, in the hills that dominate

Isiolo. We saw nothing, but a few days later the Kenya Army were more successful when they had a good contact and killed several *Shifta*. Some racial tension also flared up when a Kenya Army patrol found *Shifta* tracks leading to a residence of expatriate government employees. The latter did not report the *Shifta* visit which the Kenya Army said they were aware of, and one or two people were clubbed with rifle butts. I think the expatriates were in the wrong but I could not of course countenance the use of violence, and I was left trying to pacify both sides.

The fact that I went all night crocodile shooting with Alec Abell, Special Branch, Isiolo, and Tony, a Livestock Officer, did not escape the attention of the local DC, a Mkamba from the city, whose outlook on life was as narrow as his pointed shoes. Here we were: three expatriates on an all-night shooting expedition, in a *Shifta* infested area near Merti, without escort. The implication was that we were in league with the *Shifta*, not just three men taking a chance!

Shooting crocodile by night was exciting. We waded into the Uaso with a powerful lamp which lit up the eyes of the crocs bright red. In the process of doing so, we sometimes stepped on something very large that moved under foot. It was always a relief when the moving object turned out to be a very large catfish. Several crocodiles were bagged and Alec had them tanned in Nairobi. I was lucky in Isiolo to have two good administrators: in the late Jerry Goodman, who was ambushed by the *Shifta* at Chandlers Falls but escaped with nothing more harmful than a shot through his small pack; and Keith Taylor. Both these Inspectors managed to keep the office up to date with all the sundry chores, including signal traffic, being taken care of by themselves and without bothering me.

I was lying in bed one day feeling sorry for myself, after several aspirins had failed to curb a persistent headache, when in came Miles Oswald (nicknamed 'Tombstone' due to the prominence of his front teeth), the Assistant Commissioner in charge of the Province. He arranged for me to be admitted to Nanyuki Cottage Hospital, to which I was driven by Tony Ryan, where they diagnosed another bout of 'Tick Typhus'. I had been in the same hospital with the same complaint in 1954.

Ticks were always a nuisance. After a patrol it was usual to strip off and examine the arms and legs closely. In some areas where very small ticks that we called 'pepper ticks' predominated, it was wise to rub one's arms and legs with paraffin, before washing, to rid oneself of the scourge. Now and again a tick got through these precautionary measures and secreted itself in a spot where it could fester unhindered. If the tick had typhus, the bite would turn septic and in hospital the nurse would give you a blanket bath, hoping in the process that the water would highlight the 'sore spot'. On the first visit in 1954, the bite had been under my armpit and I visibly flinched as the water hit the sore part. On this occasion, the bite was under my scrotum, and so I made sure I did not jump when the water touched the sore!

As I was put into bed in the hospital, I was violently sick and the very pretty nurse cradled my head in her arms as she held me over a basin. At that exact moment I would rather have been left to be sick on my own, as I was in no position to appreciate my luck. How dedicated nurses are!

I was the only patient in the hospital that had four young nurses: two were Australian and two were English. The former had the latter in fits of laughter, for the Australians were reading John Hillaby's 'J-o-u-r-n-e-y t-o t-h-e J-a-d-e S-e-a', an account of the explorer's walk across the Northern Frontier to Lake Rudolph (Lake Turkana). They were all super nurses. After a couple of days the nurses asked me whether I felt strong enough to leave my bed and join them for lunch in their quarters, this would save them having to bring mine across to the hospital. I readily agreed. The following day I was asked if I felt strong enough to help them with a heavy chore. Certainly. I accompanied the two giggling English nurses who were on duty across to the mortuary where I assisted in placing a deceased American missionary into his coffin!

Several visitors came into the hospital, including 'Taffy' Vernon Roberts and the major in charge of an SAS training team. I became very friendly with the two English nurses, one of whom was from my home county of Kent and the other from Warwickshire. The latter was a gorgeous dark-haired girl who always bought me books and magazines but would never accept payment. She was so attractive that I made a determined effort not to do the obvious and fall for her. When the day came for my discharge, I asked if I might contact Isiolo to arrange for a vehicle. Gilly, the nurse in question, said that transport had already been arranged. When discharged with my overnight bag, there waiting for me was Gilly with her old VW Beetle. This delightful young lady drove me back along the dirt road to Isiolo. She captivated me and my colleagues. I can remember Terry Whitelow, of Isiolo CID, asking me who she was and the look of incredulity on his face when I proudly replied, 'My nurse.' We were very good friends for several months, driving down to Mombasa and spending a holiday there with the other English nurse and her boyfriend. Shortly afterwards, the two nurses returned to the UK on completion of their contracts.

Life in Isiolo was never going to be the same. I remember lunching with Terence Adamson, the brother of George, in his house in the hills, just a short distance from Isiolo township. When he told me that he would be quite happy to die in the Frontier and that he had no desire to go anywhere else, I realised then that I wanted to get away and that deep down I was scared that I too might get the bug to stay in the wilds. Apart from a large cobra sliding down the vines from the roof and slithering across the veranda, as we had lunch outside, the rest of the time was taken up by Terence telling me of his days with the South African troops in the Frontier during the Second World War, and how he still had details of many boreholes that the troops had dug and later on capped.

He was a fascinating man with a tremendous amount of local knowledge, much of it, I suspect, never having been committed to paper. As I gazed at him, it came to me in no uncertain manner that I wanted out.

On my next meeting with Miles Oswald I raised the prospect of a transfer and in a very short while he arranged for a change of pasture. I could go either to Nairobi, a Headquarters appointment, or Eldoret. I chose the latter as it had a large European community, English and Afrikaans, and also tribal reserves, in fact a busy district, in police terms, and one likely to offer a fresh challenge.

SEVEN

LOOK, LISTEN AND ACT

Kenya was awash with a huge variety of firearms. Some that I saw were exotic in the extreme, their value lying more in their eccentricity, than their practicability: such weapons as a combined knuckle-duster and derringer; and a twin-barrel rifle, the barrels mounted vertically, one on top of the other, one of ·22 calibre and the other ·303. These weapons were introduced into the country by the Settler population and added to by the spoils of war, ranging from the Mannlicher Carcano 7·35mm rifle and Berreta 9 mm sub-machine-gun from the Ethiopian campaign, down to the ·300 carbine from Korea. In between were Second World War relics such as the Lanchester and the Sten. Until the arrival of the Sterling SMG, it was the Sten that was the workhorse of the Kenya police, with the trusted Bren and the mortar as additional back-ups, although the latter was generally confined to GSU platoons.

The somewhat elderly 9 mm ammunition for the Sten and Sterling did not always perform well. Some said that the rounds could be stopped by a wet blanket but those that advanced this interesting theory were never around to demonstrate their trust in the blanket! There is no doubt that rounds went all over the place when fired from a Sten; but the Sterling was a great improvement both in respect of fire-power and accuracy.

The pump-action shotgun was a useful weapon in dense bush and amidst the bamboo where sometimes sub-machine-gun fire could be deflected. One soon learnt to load the shotgun (in my case a Browning) with metal cartridges as the cardboard rounds would swell up in the rain forests and jam.

During the Mau Mau emergency various 'silent' weapons were used but, generally speaking, none of the silent firearms caught on. The sub-machine-gun when fitted with a silencer made a loud clang as the bolt returned to the firing position. The large ·22 rifles, the Hornet and the Wasp, were beautifully accurate and silent but more suited to the open plain than the forest. I saw a crossbow demonstrated; it too was very silent but the bolt could easily be deflected in the forest. Some favoured the club, panga or sime and, at close quarters in the night on Pseudo operations, these were used more often than was commonly realised.

With so many firearms around, accidents were bound to happen. Pistols on the hip, where the hammer caught an obstruction and fired, killing or wounding the carrier, were not uncommon. Joyce Matcham, a settler at Ndaragwa, died in this fashion. A farmer in Nanyuki placed his ·375 heavy rifle, loaded in a sunken floor firearms safe. When he went to remove the weapon at a later date, he dropped it in the safe and the gun went off, removing most of his head. At Bernings police post we had an arms rack with a chain through the trigger guards, and it was traditional to stand well to one side when pulling the chain out to remove the weapons. One day it happened. Someone had put a loaded Greener shotgun back into the rack and as the chain was pulled out the gun went off, blowing a two-foot square hole in the roof. We were lucky to escape with slight grazes to the legs as the number 9 shot ricocheted off the mbati...

In 1954–55, several of us were entrusted with British Army issue FN (Fabrique Nationale) 7·65 mm self-loading rifles for evaluation. Whilst a weapon, to us anyway, of formidable fire-power, the weapon's main drawback was the optical sight that quickly misted up at altitude.

An outbreak of Kikuyu 'oathing' in the Rift Valley in 1962 led to field operations against the so-called Kenya Land Freedom Army (KLFA). Combined Special Branch and CID teams were set up and, in company with Jim Williams, we commenced working in the Molo District. The Director of Intelligence, Mervyn Manby, briefed me in his office above 'the carpet shop' in Kingsway, and then handed me well over £100 in cash for expenses. As I hesitated by his office door, he asked me if there was a problem. I said that I was waiting to sign for the money.

'I trust my Inspectors,' he said. I was impressed.

Jim and I had an eventful few months flogging around the Molo area with a rather sinister, 'turned' 'Oath Administrator' named 'Kenyahaho'. His information was supposed to be reliable as he had given the KLFA oath to hundreds of local Kikuyu whom he would now point out to us! In fact he was a slimy character who was using our 'cloak' to settle a few old scores. One day I caught him whipping an elderly Kikuyu woman with a bundle of stinging nettles. The beating was taking place in a *rondavel* in the grounds of Molo Police Station. I was so angry that it is possible that I may have injured his pride, as I whacked him with my baton.

In company with Jim, who provided the CID expertise when court action was required, the extent of the KLFA octopus was unravelled and various home-made guns and other weapons recovered from caches. In moments of relaxation, we played snooker with Len Wenman in his 'Wenman's' hotel in Molo, which Len always won as we played in the dark. Len always reckoned that it was too light to switch the generator on! Our investigations were interrupted when an African servant brained a European male in Molo township with a charcoal iron, after the two had a row. Jim took over the murder inquiry.

Jim was an ex-Metropolitan police officer as was his wife, Joan, whom I think, as a sergeant, outranked her husband. Joan told me of an adventure in the 'Met' when she was acting as a decoy in an attempt to catch a rapist in Greenwich. Apparently she was on one side of a high wall and her escort on the other; when she needed the protection, her escort had difficulty in trying to scale the wall!

When not engaged in 'bundu bashing', my attachment to Special Branch Headquarters, Nairobi, was with the Surveillance Section. Initially the section was commanded by John Pilkington, an Anglo-Portugese, who strangely enough, although fairly proficient in English and Portugese, could never master more than a rudimentary knowledge of Kiswahili. John sort of hovered round the Chief Inspector rank because of this, and when he went on leave, I borrowed the rank until his return. Alongside me was Derek Harris, a quiet but far from ineffectual officer, who had other irons in the fire, including the writing of short stories.

Operationally we had a total strength of about thirty men, there were no female officers and I shudder to think of the problems we might have had, had there been any ladies in the teams, for sometimes the car crews could be huddled together for long hours during the night, when windows would have been well misted up and temptation rife. To support the foot surveillance teams, we had, at the best times, some half a dozen mixed vehicles, bicycles and the odd motor scooter. All the vehicles and bicycles had radios, which were linked to the surveillance headquarters which, in those days was situated near the main Nairobi post office. The post office was also a rendezvous for the then clandestine meetings of the homosexual fraternity, which provided some light-hearted amusement, and a few raised eyebrows when familiar faces appeared, for the Operations Room staff.

The section was not affluent enough to be able to afford the renting of 'Static Observation Points', although we did share some offices with the agent-running section which had been well used and were probably 'blown'. In the early days we had licensed tea sellers who would dispense chai on street corners where their command of view would be advantageous to Special Branch, but in later years this ploy was terminated, as the African 'other ranks' found the job onerous, particularly during the rains.

The section was deployed against both internal organisations and individuals, of varying sophistication; and foreign elements, both visiting and resident in Kenya. Usually, but not always, the targets tended to be from the 'Left'.

The vicissitudes of surveillance work are well known. One good identification of a contact has to be counter-balanced against the many hours of frustration and boredom. One evening a Somali target was receiving our attention in Nairobi city centre. A Somali of interest was seen to drive his car away from his office and park the vehicle near the Kenya Cinema at the bottom end of Government road. Here he caught a taxi and returned to the centre of town where he 'lurked'. A European drove up, glanced at the Somali and then parked his car. The European caught a taxi and drove away and the Somali walked off round the block where one of the three cars on duty spotted him getting into the taxi with the European we had sighted earlier. Surely there was some international intrigue afoot here? Not at all! The European turned out to be Chief Inspector Peter Laycock of Special Branch, who was no doubt advancing the cause of the forces of law and order.

During the days of the 'Kiama Kia Muingi' (Society of the People) a Kikuyu organisation aiming to get quicker control of land for the people, the Surveillance section were tasked to follow a leading activist on his release from custody. Now, the Kikuyu will always plot; and land, a most emotive subject in Africa, is always top of the list of their grievances. Even as I write some Kikuyu will be forming another organisation to overthrow their own government; they cannot help it, the desire to plot is endemic.

The target was Hezikiah 'Tumbo' ('Tummy') Mwai, who was released from Nyeri Prison. The section had never operated outside Nairobi for more than a day or so and this operation was to be played 'by ear'. 'Tumbo' came out of prison and was followed by foot teams, who rode in the same mini-buses as he skirted the Aberdares, taking three days to reach Nakuru via Thompsons Falls (Nyahururu). How we would have coped had he walked over the Aberdare Mountains, is a matter of conjecture.

William Kivuvani and myself set ourselves up in the Stag's Head Hotel, Nakuru, where we ran the operation for one week, trying to identify and photograph all Tumbo's *rafikis* (friends). In the hotel William and I encountered a lot of inquisitive questioning from the staff who wanted to know what an African and European were doing dining together, day after day. They were told that we were from Williams Diamond Mines in Tanganyika, and that we hoped to set up an office in Nakuru. We were amused, too! The operation was 75 per cent successful, but had to be curtailed when a barman from the 'Amigos' club, a former Pseudo of mine, saw me and came to the hotel to ask for a reference.

Never a technical man and having no technical expertise, it was however quite common for the Surveillance section to be called upon to provide some sort of support for technical operations. This could range from providing a *cordon sanitaire* around the target or target premises to escorting the technical officer in and out of a job. Some operations led to incidents; not always amusing at the time, but on reflection, absolutely hilarious. Bob Carman, one of our technical officers, was a truly scientific bod, never happier than when he was immersed in chemicals or surrounded by a myriad of strange wires. He was also very absent-minded.

We had gained entry to a hotel room and Bob set his case on the floor whilst he searched for the key. He had mislaid it! But in his pocket he had a small screwdriver and he said that he could pick the suitcase lock with no bother at all. Unfortunately, whilst so engaged the screwdriver slipped and cut his wrist so badly that I was frantically mopping up the blood from the carpet, whilst Bob tried to stem the flow. All was not lost and the clandestine entry so stood, although I did ponder on whether next time I should take a first aid kit with me.

En route to the then new Nairobi Airport at Embakasi, in a car with Bob, Dick Crow and Bob Culff, to carry out another of Bob's technical tasks, there was a dreadful stench in the car which resulted in much eye contact and actual lowering of the car windows. At the airport, whilst Bob was about his nefarious task in his shirt-sleeves, Bob Culff identified Bob Carman's sports jacket as being the source of the stench. It seemed to have been soaked in some powerful chemical. The jacket in question was whipped away and locked in a filing cabinet. We returned to headquarters with Bob minus his jacket and I suspect that he has not missed it to this day!

We had a host of briefcases, handbags and filing boxes fitted with robot cameras that, before the days of battery motors, were wound up by hand. These, and many other bits and pieces, were the work of Jasper Maskelyne, a member of the Magic Circle who served in the Special Operations Executive (SOE) during the Second World War.

There was an extremely competent technical officer working in the Weights and Measures Department, Nairobi, who assisted our operations from time to time. The officer, whose name I think was Phillips, was said to have managed to secure audio evidence that led to a conviction, whilst he and the subject he was trying to entrap were riding a motor cycle.

Bob Carman had a sports car, an Alpine I think, and he used one of the Surveillance *godowns* in the industrial area in which to tinker with his car. Having been working on the vehicle one morning, he broke off from his labours to accompany John Pilkington and myself to make some enquiries. As we headed back to base later that day, we were overtaken by a couple of fire engines that were heading towards a pall of black smoke. Needless to say, when we reached the godowns, there was Bob's Alpine gutted by fire! There were of course many other amusing incidents, but to describe them, even after all this time, would be to touch on matters that best remain in the minds of the participants, and not aired in public . . .

Sometimes, usually of an evening, it was necessary to provide female support for surveillance teams if the target settled down in a hotel bar or a restaurant for a meal. It was usual to call upon volunteers from the secretarial staff at Special Branch Headquarters. I can recall Pam Carson (now Newton) and Shirley Brown (now Holyoak) being so deployed. Pam, a relative of George Adamson, was called out one night to provide additional cover for John Pilkington and myself. We were attending to two Red Chinese visitors to Kenya, in the 'Pagoda' restaurant at the bottom end of Government Road. The two Chinese had ordered their meal as we called for Pam, and as she arrived in the 'Pagoda' in anticipation of a good supper, the two visitors bolted their bowls of boiled rice and took off smartly for their next appointment. It was not always so, sometimes the ladies had time to enjoy a meal and also take note of events of interest to the Branch.

The section were frequent visitors to the airport, usually picking up incoming persons of interest, homing them to a hotel or residence, and then going on from there. There was always a lot of hanging around to do, both at hotels and the airport. To provide better cover for the latter, I was gazetted as an Immigration Officer, and authorised to enter the customs area and arrival hall. Those not in the know thought that I had in fact transferred to the Immigration Department, as did one of my football-playing colleagues, Noel Maynard. On several occasions I was approached at the airport, usually I must admit, by large and loud American matrons who mistakenly thought that I was the 'White Hunter' waiting to take them on their safari.

There was a particularly bothersome branch of the Kenya African National Union (KANU) Youth Wing in Nairobi, and the section was briefed to identify all those entering or leaving the Youth Wing premises. Now, it is a well-known fact that throughout Africa Youth Wing can be a misleading title, as many of the members are close to approaching pensionable age!

This particular branch was noted for its thuggery, and as the site of the Youth Wing office was in an area of open grassland with just a few ramshackle huts, there being virtually no natural cover, any white presence was likely to attract more than just a passing glance.

After a liaison visit to the Department of Surveys, we set out to survey the large grass area right opposite the Youth Wing office. Our small squad of five men marched around with small red-and-white painted poles looking, we hoped, professional as I took sightings through the 'theodolite', that was mounted on a pukka tripod. The theodolite housed a robot camera and telephoto lens, by kind permission of Jasper, that actually took photographs through the side of the casing. One could therefore take sight on a pole dead ahead, looking well away from the office and, with the aid of well-angled internal lenses, keep the door of the office in sight and activate the camera when a body entered or left. We accumulated two days' 'take' before deciding that that particular ploy was best brought to an end. There was only one rumble during this period, and this occurred when the 'man on the door' came over to ask what was going on. He was told that the Nairobi Council was considering building a dog racing track on the site . . . and that's how rumours start.

During the run-up to internal self-government, other rumours began to spread around Nairobi of a possible white insurrection. Various local newspapers were informed that weapons were being assembled and that uniforms for the alleged dissidents had been ordered. Special Branch investigations of various types were instigated and the sole culprit, a disaffected brother of a serving Special Branch officer, was identified and warned off. Although only a pin-prick, there was always the possibility of the 'threat' getting out of hand at the moment of Kenya's first move towards total independence. I was once asked by some white settlers, a couple of years prior to the events described above, where the Kenya Police would stand if the settlers ever tried to take matters in their own hands. I believe that they correctly anticipated my own reply, which was: they would support the Government.

To provide the Surveillance Section with new blood, recruits were sought from outside the Police Force and taken on two-year contracts. The King's African Rifles (KAR), later to become the Kenya Army, had a resettlement board who were approached for potential 'recruits'. At a safe office within view of the New Stanley Hotel, John Pilkington and myself interviewed a selection of retired senior NCOs; a couple were former Warrant Officers and very impressive they were too. Those selected were put under training for a couple of weeks to test their suitability. Their initial brief, until they were accepted for further training, was that they would be working for a private company as security personnel, which would involve them following persons suspected of theft or hire purchase fraud, for example. All very basic; but at the end of the two weeks we had our new men and they then joined the section and were allowed into our various offices to continue with in-house training. The question of their vetting was comparatively easy as we had access to their Army records. The men worked well for many years; but as is so often the case in Africa, tribalism reared up and the civilians were disbanded.

Alongside the Surveillance Section Operations Room, there was an efficient Secretarial Unit. Various wives of serving police officers worked there, one of whom was Irene Hughes;

but the mainstay over the years was a mature English 'gentle-woman' Dorothy Hogg, a former resident of Rumuruti. She retired to England but died on a holiday in Kenya and is buried at Langatta cemetery. Dorothy, a lovely lady, was also efficient and discreet.

Technical operations were usually exciting because of the constant possibility of being either disturbed or at the worst 'rumbled'. As a supporting officer, I would watch with some interest as holes were drilled and microphones inserted, or perhaps a leg removed from a table and replaced with an identical item that came ready equipped with a device and the batteries to power the thing. These were the days before we had electric movers, so it was necessary to pack as much battery power as possible into the device, otherwise there would be a requirement to return to the scene again to replace the power unit. Sometimes I would act as monitor in a nearby location, checking that the wire-recorder was functioning and, where necessary, setting up an indoor aerial to improve reception. There were naturally near misses and some close shaves; but as far as I am aware, no one was ever caught red-handed.

On one occasion we were looking after a visitor of European origin. I was in the next bedroom when the visitor was called upon by a colleague in Special Branch who was a friend. The colleague caught sight of me leaving the bedroom and, quite naturally put two and two together. There was a feeling amongst my other colleagues that the operation had been blown. There was certainly room for greater liaison amongst Special Branch officers to prevent this sort of incident arising, and I recall that some fur flew amongst those officers who were senior to me.

The arrival of the Eastern bloc Diplomatic Missions with attendant fellow travellers such as the Novosti Press, Pravda and the New China News Agency, gave the Surveillance Section and others in Special Branch a lot more work. There is no doubt that the Soviets and the Chinese found the identification of the African watchers difficult. Our weakness was in the vehicle area as, having only a half dozen vehicles to play with, it was very difficult to modify them sufficiently to pull the wool over the eyes of a trained intelligence officer. In the city centre, with attendant traffic jams, life was easier for the foot and bike teams.

We had an Israeli intelligence officer in transit from a neighbouring country, and I sought to keep my hand in by covertly photographing him myself. Whenever I moved in towards him, he turned away. It was apparent that I should have left the job to one of my African colleagues, who would have blended in the jostling crowds more easily but having gone so far, I was determined to carry on and actually ended up going inside a shop in Government Road, and snapping the Israeli as he was 'window shopping'. I got the impression that he was more intent in looking at the reflection than the goods in the window!

On another occasion a team retrieved a pornographic magazine left by a Russian in a hotel lavatory. The magazine, which contained a number of large ink dots, was sent to the lab for analysis. The lab staff said that they found the magazine interesting and could we get another one? Was there any security interest, we asked? Oh no they replied, we just took a fancy to it!

The combined CID–Special Branch mail interception unit, located near the Gardens Hotel, picked up mail of interest to CID in the criminal context and to Special Branch in the subversive sphere. At one time the CID officer was Ivan King, GM, a former Metropolitan Police officer. Ivan showed me some Scandinavian magazines with full frontal male nudes in glorious technicolour.

'Are they to be burnt?' I enquired.

'Oh no,' said Ivan, 'I place them in the post-boxes of single ladies.'

Of course he was joking. I think.

In conjunction with the Army Air Corps, the Section experimented with the use of Beaver light aircraft and a helicopter in carrying out surveillance work. Events had shown, that in the vast open plains surrounding Nairobi (i.e. the Nairobi National Game Park) surveillance vehicles, with their ever constant plumes of dust, found it difficult to track those persons of security interest, such as Foreign Intelligence Officers who opted to meet their contacts under the guise of game watching.

The Beaver, in radio contact with cars well back from the target vehicle(s), was a brilliant success. It was only unfortunate that the first identification was an innocent one; a senior Government official (Malcolm MacDonald, the British High Commissioner) who met up with a Chinese lady. Both had an interest in birds.

The helicopter, although noisy, proved useful in the Limuru area where the pilot could fly down a neighbouring valley without being noticed or heard from the ground but being able to keep sight of a target vehicle on the next ridge.

My previous experience of an Army Air Corps helicopter was in evacuating a wounded man from the NFD, when the pilot took the wrong cut-line and flew along the border with Somalia (with the wounded man encapsulated in a pod underneath) until he ran out of fuel. There was a race to refuel the machine, having only a hand-pump and a drum of aviation fuel, before the other side got on the scene. We did manage . . . It always surprised me how junior the pilots were, both in years and rank. They certainly had a lot of nerve in flying solo in the NFD, for their fuel capacity did not allow for much error.

The Chinese Embassy in Nairobi, which was surrounded by a high brick wall, was the subject of much interest when they began to undertake a considerable amount of re-building within the Embassy compound. As one of several ploys to discover what exactly was going on, a fresh-faced Special Branch officer dressed in a Boy Scout's uniform was sent in to volunteer to do some car washing, under the 'Bob-a-Job' banner. A somewhat taken aback Chinese official opened the door and indicated to our man that he should wait until an interpreter arrived. A person competent in English duly appeared and was told about the 'Bob-a-Job' task, and did the Embassy have any cars to clean?

'Bugger off,' came the Chinese reply!

In addition to keeping an eye on local subversives and the esoteric Foreign Intelligence Officers, the section was also briefed, both shortly before and after Independence, to check on the activities of several senior African politicians whose trustworthiness was not fully established. This was a tricky area in which to operate, as some of the gentlemen concerned had lots of attendant hangers-on ('eyes'), who made the going very difficult.

One such senior figure soon became aware that he was being tailed. He would motor up Valley Road, indicate that he was turning right, and then turn left. Needless to say, such violations of the Highway Code were hardly compatible with his esteemed position (law was his discipline) and the operation was discontinued.

One of the local 'left wing' targets, a Goan by the name of Pinto, ran a private printing business in the Nairobi industrial area. We latched on to him from time to time, to see what he was up to. Having withdrawn his attendant watchers one week, to concentrate on another more pressing target, some political assassins gunned him down as he drove into his Westlands home in his white, two-stroke Saab.

Another unusual assignment was to assist with the protection of Sir Roy Welensky at Nairobi Airport, when the visiting Prime Minister stopped off to meet Kenya officials in the VIP lounge. There was a report of uncertain credibility that hinted at the possibility of an attempted assassination. Apart from scrutinising some journalists on the observation terrace, who were rummaging around with various telephoto lenses, my small part in the affair and only contact with Sir Roy was when he left the VIP lounge by the wrong door: confronted by myself, he commented, 'I can see this is not the Gents'.'

One of the surveillance team drivers, 'Simba' (lion) by name, had an aptitude for private enterprise. A short and stocky individual, he was also a taxi driver for a large Nairobi company, an arrangement that was most beneficial to the section as Simba could be directed to a target under natural cover, acting as his guardian for the duration of the hire. Simba also had connections with 'vehicle mechanics' in the River Road area of Nairobi, where it was possible to buy vehicle spares at rock-bottom prices, as they were usually stolen from vehicles, including the purchasers', a few days previously.

One day, Simba, who had got into our bad books by having the crankshaft of a privately purchased surveillance vehicle welded only for it to blow up shortly afterwards, resigned from the Kenya Police and embarked on a countrywide safari with an American matron of some means. The relationship developed and Simba left for the USA in company with his new lady, where she bought him a large car and settled him into her home. But the call of Africa beckoned and, after a few months Simba returned home, bought himself a new car and amused his Wkamba contemporaries in the drinking dens of Nairobi with stories of life for an African in the United States.

Shortly before Tanganyika became Tanzania, we had a liaison visit from officers of the Tanganyika Special Branch who were in the process of setting up a more sophisticated surveillance section and had come to Nairobi to avail themselves of our expertise and experience in dealing with a wider range of targets. The Kenya Police had advanced both in training and equipment largely due to the Mau Mau emergency, and I believe we were able to assist our East African colleagues.

Shifting to the plateau of the Uasin Gishu was like a good breath of fresh air. Eldoret was a thriving farming area with a large expatriate population, an active Town Council, a Mayor, light industry, and the nearby Nandi Reserve. In addition Eldoret sat astride the main Uganda–Nairobi road.

There were still many Afrikaaners in residence, mainly on the farms and small-holdings, although some of their number had started the 'reverse trek' back to South Africa, complete with their heavily-laden lorries and trucks.

There were growing problems of African squatters on expatriate farms particularly, but not solely, on those with absent owners. Stock theft was rampant; as was the unauthorised movement of undipped stock by local tribesmen which caused great anguish to European farmers, many of whom had pedigree stock to protect. Word came from 'the top', that no action should be taken against squatters, as long as they were not committing theft or similar, as to move them on would be politically unacceptable to the KANU government. One began to notice changes on the ground as those that had recently acquired positions of authority, started to use power for their own purposes. Government lorries were seen to be visiting farms on private journeys, often laden on both legs of the trip, with the drivers willingly telling us the name of the Minister, Permanent Secretary or other senior government official that they were working for.

When I took over the reins from my predecessor, Willy De Beer, he gave me the only key to a back door, leading from the Divisional Commanders' office, to be used in times of emergency! I laughingly accepted it, not realising how there would be a real need to use the back door until a couple of expatriate pests, who still refused to deal with an African police officer, plagued me with daily visits.

At my first meeting with the Town Council the question of prostitution was raised and I feel some people were not pleased when I pointed out that a demand must exist, otherwise the ladies would not be there. In common with most towns, the problem is still there and likely to remain but we did try to move them on from the main shopping area, much the same as police forces the world over.

Once fighting began in Buganda, there were a flood of refugees, some of them with arms, crossing into Kenya and making their way to Nairobi. Road-blocks were set up to monitor the influx, with particular attention to the infiltration of arms.

At 2 a.m. one of the roadblocks reported that they had opened fire on a car that had sped through the red stop lights (since the barriers were on the roadside!) but that the vehicle and occupants had got away unharmed. The incident remained a mystery for six years. It was solved when I heard a forest officer in the Maseru Club in Lesotho, telling a party of drinking cronies of his exploits in Kenya which included being fired upon in Eldoret!

He told me his story. He had been driving from Kitale to Nairobi when he saw some red lights on the road. He slowed down but as there was no one around, he sped off. As he worked up speed again, he heard some shots and thought he was being ambushed by bandits, so he accelerated away as fast as he could. His implication was that if it was a roadblock, the police were asleep. The same person was abducted by guerrillas in Mozambique a few months later, and his name was in the

national press as he endured a long march before he was
released.

Although I was the only European police officer in the
Division, I did have the reassuring presence of Don Thompson
to sort out any problems with the communications network:
Chief Inspector Alexander, my second-in-command, an able
administrator; Des Mair the Quartermaster, a shy, but efficient
man; Parminder Baraj, a Crime Branch officer, who went on to
command Tambach Police Station; and Harry Jassy who
commanded Burnt Forest Police Station with a minimum of
fuss. These last three officers put an extra item on the lunch at
my wedding (a delicious curry) when I married Jenny, a
teacher at Highlands School, Eldoret, in April 1966. Jenny has
been at my side ever since.

When inspecting Eldama Ravine Police Post, I was fascinated
and saddened to read in the Officers' Visiting Book, which
went back to the 1950s, of the tragic confrontation with an
extremist religious sect, Dini Ya Msambwa ('Religion of the
Spirits of the Departed'), that took place in April 1950. A
combined police and administration force were confronted by
some 500 armed Suk members of the DYM. As the lives of the
Government forces were in grave danger, the senior police
officer present gave the order to open fire. Unfortunately the
order was countermanded by the District Commissioner and
the Suk were allowed to get too close before he relented and
urged the police to open fire.

In the ensuing battle two expatriate police officers, one
District Officer and one Tribal Police corporal were killed. The
tragic entry in the Officers' Visiting Book recorded the collection of the personal effects of the late Assistant Inspector R. G.
Cameron, one of the police officers killed, who had only
recently arrived at Eldama Ravine. One of the welcome aspects
of the universal adult franchise in the first election held in
February 1961, was that under the Federal Constitution (which
did not last for long!) the Kenya Police at long last took over the
responsibility for law and order.

Directly opposite the Divisional Police Headquarters in Eldoret, a small travel agent's was run almost single-handed by a stout and elderly European lady. She drove a Morris Minor to and from her home, a matter of a mile or so each way, in second gear accompanied by clouds of smoke and much revving at road junctions. The Traffic Section asked me if I could have a word with the lady about her poor standard of driving and almost total disregard for the 'rule of the road'. It seemed she was too formidable for them!

One evening I waved her down. She waved back at me and sped off in a cloud of black smoke, the engine screaming in maximum revs. I followed her home and had a few gentle words with her. The car had only one forward gear that was operative and she did not think the vehicle worth repairing. I was able to persuade her otherwise. As I was leaving, she came over to my staff car and looked at the new Police badge where the Latin 'Salus Populi' (Servants of the People) had been replaced by the Kiswahili 'Utumishi Kwa Wote'. Did this mean, the old lady said, that there would now be cooks for all? (The Swahili for 'cook' is 'Mpishi' and 'Kwa Wote' is 'for all'.) I was lost for words.

Jenny and I left Eldoret (and Kenya) in 1966, when we drove overland to Cape Town. I was the last expatriate Divisional Commander. Established records that went back to 1927 placed Captain E. K. Catchpole as the first. It was sad to leave '64' (the number allocated to Eldoret by the Land Survey Department in the early nineteenth century, which has stuck). But we had the excitement of the Great North Road to tackle, southwards through the highlands of Tanzania, Zambia and the 'breakaway' Rhodesia, where we were to find a graveyard of heavy lorries overturned on the dirt roads ... but that is another story.

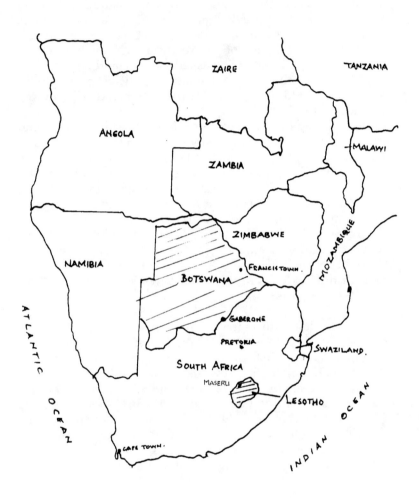

EIGHT

BAHRAIN
BASUTOLAND (LESOTHO)
AND BOTSWANA

It was Ian Henderson who arranged for me to join forces with him in the Bahrain Special Branch. The recruitment was swift and facilitated from within the SB, for after I had been in post for several weeks, the British Political Agent, Tony Parsons (later Sir Anthony Parsons, the British Delegate to the United Nations), called me to his office to tell me that my medical had been arranged in London!

Bahrain, whose name means 'two seas', is an archipelago of small low-lying islands about fifteen miles from the Arabian coast and centrally situated in the Gulf, of which Bahrain, the largest, measures thirty miles long by nine miles wide. Apart from a narrow cultivated strip along the northern coast, the interior is mainly desolate and barren desert. As oil was discovered and produced as far back as 1932, Bahrain has been able to develop its economy much earlier than neighbouring Gulf sheikdoms, although the bulk of the oil is now exhausted and there is more reliance on the production of natural gas.

Bahrain, like most small islands, can be claustrophobic. One felt that one was at the centre of Middle East intrigue, although once outside the island a sense of the rational returned and with it the realisation that in fact the island was little more than a back water in political terms, although its strategic value in military terms is somewhat greater.

As is the case with the Eastern Province of Saudi Arabia, Bahrain has a substantial Shiite population, although the ruling family are Sunni. The Shia have a tendency to look externally for political and spiritual leads, and from time to time this manifests itself in riots and other forms of discontent.

The previous Special Branch regime had been severely disrupted when two of the senior officers, Bob Langdale and Ahmed Mohsin, had been blown up and injured by car bombs. It was with some satisfaction that several years after the event, Inspector Yousif Ishaq and myself led the team that brought the bomber to justice. The culprit, a fellow-traveller of the NLF, was a most unlikely terrorist. He had a lot of African blood in him, smoked marijuana and was a jazz musician. He had learnt his other skill in Egypt under the Nasser regime.

In general terms the island was peaceful. There was an active National Liberation Front (NLF), a home-grown left-wing organisation that was something of a nuisance in that they distributed leaflets attacking the ruling family. The NLF was eventually broken by Special Branch, with the assistance of another Gulf state, and then closely monitored by another ex-Kenya colleague, Superintendent Brian Shore.

Unlike Brian who persevered with his spoken Arabic, my knowledge was really confined to those Swahili words that have Arabic origins. I relied upon a Jordanian officer, with whom I worked in tandem. A Roman Catholic who at one time was training for the priesthood, who had some scandalous tales to tell of the artifacts manufactured for the pilgrims in Jerusalem, Abu Liyha (not his real name) was a good companion and we roamed the islands together, at all hours, on various investigations.

Bahrain was party to the Arab boycott of Jewish goods, and for a time there was the irritation of having to remove labels such as Marks and Spencers from clothing and the Customs were also hot on records that bore the name of a company that had Jewish connections or traded with Israel. It was therefore something of a victory over the system to be singing 'Born is the King of Israel' at a carol service in St Christopher's Anglican Church in Manama, until a Seychelles lady, who had started her celebrations early, was violently sick all over my back as I knelt down praying. I had to leave the church to wash my jacket under the garden tap; even so, when I returned to my pew, Jenny and I had the whole row to ourselves. Jenny and Celia Shore provided some of the expertise needed to card the complex Arab names in the Special Branch Registry indexes.

There were other moments of light relief, such as bathing my young daughter Nicky at the age of 11 months, in a freshwater spring that bubbles up from the depths of the saline waters of the sea. I am told that the water probably originates from the mountains of Iran. At a private audience with the Ruler, Sheikh Eissa bin Sulman Al Khalifa, when he congratulated me on the birth of my daughter ('She can always have a Bahraini passport'), he said that Arabs regard daughters as 'mistakes' such is the desire for male progeny. Jenny thought this very amusing as does Nicky who is now a police officer.

Some additional light relaxation was obtained by visiting Ralph Izzard, the Daily Telegraph Foreign Correspondent. We sat on scatter cushions and were cooled in the heat and high humidity of a Gulf summer by the breezes that trickled down from the wind towers. Ralph was something of a bohemian figure who did not always see eye to eye with officialdom, although those that knew him well respected him. With a background in Naval Intelligence, he had travelled widely and covered many of the world's trouble spots including Kenya, Cyprus and Korea. It was through Ralph that I became aware of wider developments in the Gulf which interested both of us.

Lesotho (Basutoland before the country gained independence in 1966) is a largely mountainous country situated in the midst of South Africa, so that entrance to or exit from Lesotho is made on South African roads or via their airspace.

Arriving in Maseru in August 1971, when I took over from Ted Irvine, a former Malawi Police officer who went on to Cambridge and then Hong Kong, one was immediately conscious of the stranglehold that South Africa could, and sometimes did, impose on the small mountainous kingdom.

Lesotho's internal politics were split into two main groups which perhaps not so strangely, also reflected the religious divide between Roman Catholics and Anglicans; plus a Royalist party that supported King Moshoeshoe II, and a tiny Communist Party. The Basuto are frenzied in their political affiliation and the activists in either of the two main parties would not countenance the right of their opponents to even exist; and when the opportunity came for scores to be settled, they were carried out without any mercy.

The country had held democratic elections in the previous year and as the counting got alarmingly close to a defeat for the ruling Basutoland National Party (BNP), headed by the Prime Minister Chief Leabua Jonathan, the latter, with support from various government officials, declared a state of emergency, and suspended the constitution.

The Director of Intelligence, Tony Burney, a former Northern Rhodesian police officer, later proudly told me that he and several other senior expatriate colleagues who had supported Chief Jonathan's suspension of the constitution were known as the 'dirty dozen'. Tony and his delightful but unassuming wife, Yvonne, put me up for a few days until I was allocated a house, when plans for my family to join me could be made.

As Flight Officer Yvonne Baseden of the WAAF, Yvonne worked for the SOE (F) section during the Second World War: parachuted into France, captured and tortured at Ravensbruck, she was awarded the MBE (M) and the Croix de Guerre avec Palme. Although Yvonne never mentioned her experiences, I was pleased to see her photograph on the wall by the staircase at the Special Forces Club in London.

Assisting Tony were two other former Northern Rhodesian police officers: Frank Cook in Maseru; and Tony Petts who was stationed a couple of hours' car ride north at Leribe.

As Deputy Head of Intelligence, my role was that of a Headquarters officer who supervised the writing of the weekly intelligence summary to the Cabinet and, along with the Director, supervising and directing officers in the field. The work was very parochial and although it was the life-blood of my local colleagues, to an expatriate the intelligence collected was trivial and boring. Opposition politics were marginally more interesting than those of the ruling party; but only just. A slight glimmer of interest was aroused by incursions from across the border, both by the security forces and the liberation organisations.

South African penetration of Lesotho was carried out at every level from humble village headmen up to senior government officials. Indeed some of my local colleagues were on the South African payroll. South African officers from the Police Security Branch and the Bureau of State Security (BOSS) roamed throughout the length and breadth of Lesotho, treating the country as if it were a province of South Africa. They moved around with confidence and conceit, in a mixture of interviewing-cum-debriefing, as they passed from one Government office to another. Some of the tales related to me by the SAP (SB) personnel of their activities in their own country were really quite terrifying. They were the law, judge and worse. It was wise not to turn one's back on them, even on a bright sunny day.

The BOSS officers were more cultured and perhaps less sinister, but equally as active, particularly in the early 1970s, in criss-crossing the Mountain Kingdom. They did interfere in local politics and lost money in trying to fund one of the smaller groups. There were of course many legitimate targets for the South Africans for Lesotho harboured refugees from the African National Congress (ANC) and the Pan African Congress (PAC). Both groups were heavily infiltrated and, if six refugees got together for a political meeting, we would attempt to hazard a guess at the identity of the only one who was not working for the South Africans!

Subsistence farming in the mountains of Lesotho was precarious and when the crops failed, more and more Basuto went to work in the South African gold mines. It was simple for the South Africans to sieve through the names of the workers for people who might be of use to them at some date or other. Chief Jonathan himself was a 'pit boss' in the gold mines and must have come to South African notice early in his political career.

Because he sensed that the South Africans did not respect him, Sahalahala Solomon Molapo, who succeeded Tony Burney as

Director of Intelligence, asked me to carry out the bulk of the liaison duties with them. Sahalahala was one of the old school who had risen through the ranks. He was the most honest of all the African officers I dealt with, so much so that he would present me with the Special Branch funds every month, leaving me to allocate them, so that his compatriots could not point the finger at him for misappropriation of funds.

The liaison duties, conducted both in Lesotho and various places in South Africa, led to some lively and very interesting exchanges. An official liaison group of South African police were one day giving us details of the successes they had achieved, through the use of police dogs, in searching large numbers of 'non-whites' in locations and townships for arms and drugs. When I asked how the Muslems amongst the 'coloured' population reacted to being sniffed by dogs, the Inspector said that the dogs did not discriminate. They would bite anyone!

Efforts were made to induce closer cooperation on my part. Knowing our mutual liking for a *braaivlais* (barbecue), my main opponent, known as Gys, would firstly offer me some steak promising that next time he would bring a whole sheep or half a steer. When I protested that I would be unable to keep such a large quantity of meat, Gys would then suggest that he be allowed to provide me with a deep-freeze, and so on.

On the credit side he was certainly not a thug. I stayed with him and his family in their Pretoria home and accompanied Gys and a colleague to watch the British Lions rugby team draw with the Free State in Bloemfontein.

Gys had a well-developed sense of humour. He told me that his English had improved since we began our meetings, and how this would upset his father if he ever found out. It would seem his father was alive at the time of the Boer War and, in Gys' own words, 'He was inoculated against the British with a bully-beef tin!'

In spite of the South Africans' continued watch on my movements and the undoubted suborning of some of my junior staff, we did succeed more than once in tweaking the springbok tail by recording some of their agent meetings and sending them ready-made agents.

*

Lesotho's mountainous terrain has seen many a skirmish between Basutho tribesmen and the soldiers of Queen Victoria, but the Boer War was fought largely around the country's borders, with Lesotho escaping the conflict and acting as a supply base for the British, mainly by supplying the sturdy Basutho ponies for remounts. At Mount Moroosi I did see a lone grave of a British trooper whose death was recorded in 1819, the grave having been prepared by the Boers. It was also said that many of the telephone lines that snaked up and down the mountains, which were still working in the 1970s, had in fact been erected by British sappers in the early 1900s.

Our man at Leribe, Tony Petts, had a national monument in his garden, and that was a well-preserved rondavel authenticated as having been lived in by General ('Chinese') Gordon.

Delving in the archives revealed that Lord Kitchener of Khartoum, himself a Worshipful Brother, had provided the escort for the warrant authorising the founding of the Masonic Lodge in Basutoland in March 1902, after the previous warrant was intercepted and destroyed by the Boers in 1899. Nothing changes!

BOSS officers were wary of the Masonic Lodge and I know that they kept a check on South Africans visiting the Maseru lodge and vice versa. Just over the South African border at Riverside there was a meeting hall ('shell-hole') of the 'MOTHS' (Memorable Order of Tin Hats), an organisation that is strong on the ground throughout the more 'English' areas of South Africa. The South African Afrikaaner, particularly those in the security services, found some of these British organisations perplexing. I can remember with amusement the embarrassed look on the face of a BOSS officer who wanted to know whether I had ever come across the organisation that he was investigating by the name of 'TOCH'. I told him about the lack of light from the lamp.

The Prime Minister, Chief Leabua Jonathan, called all his senior civil servants together from time to time, usually to give them a pep-talk. At one such gathering he announced his intention to change the police ranks to their military equivalents (in line with South Africa) as to his mind 'Superintendents' were associated with hospitals. This command was duly carried out and we became captains, majors and colonels etc.

At another meeting Chief Jonathan held forth about the generally poor state of the government hospitals and health centres. He said that most people went to the Mission hospitals for treatment (this was true, Jenny had our second child, Wendy, at Roma Mission hospital, as the government hospitals were usually out of drugs, oxygen etc.). In the Prime Minister's opinion, extensive theft from the hospitals by civil servants left a dearth of medical drugs and equipment. He went on to say that if there was a 'theft event' at the Olympic Games, Lesotho would undoubtedly win a few gold medals!

On an even more disturbing note, there were the signs of discontent within the Police Mobile Unit (PMU), which was later to become the Army. A middle-ranking expatriate police officer, who could speak Sesotho, came to us with tales he had heard from the 'young captains', who wanted greater power, more money and the right to hunt down opposition political figures. When the Opposition Basutoland Congress Party (BCP) attempted a clumsy coup d'état in the early 1970s, the PMU exacted revenge by widespread killing, much of which took place inside buildings such as police stations. The command of the PMU eventually passed to a local officer, Justin Lekhanya (with whom I had a reasonable rapport), who as a 'General' was eventually to overthrow his own Prime Minister.

The appointment of a local Commissioner of Police became more viable with the posting of an expatriate Police Advisor to Lesotho. The man chosen was J. I. 'Bob' Burns, CBE, an experienced officer who had served in the Indian Army, the police forces of Malaya and Tanganyika, and who had been Commissioner in the Gulf State of Sharja. Bob was to prove his worth by helping to steer the locals away from the excesses that they craved to follow and by beefing up the top administration of the Lesotho Mounted Police (LMP) which had been allowed to deteriorate. Another welcome arrival was John K. Lawrence as Transport Officer. John, a former Northern Rhodesian police officer, came from a police background as his father, Jesse, was at one time Chief Constable of Reading.

The Lesotho Mounted Police have a post at Sani Pass where the four-wheel drive track dips down alarmingly, at a gradient of 1 in $2^1/_2$, to the Natal Province of South Africa. The post was sited on a large outcrop of rock, somewhere in the region of 3,000 metres above sea-level, in the Drakensberg Mountains not far from southern Africa's highest peak, Thabantlenyana at 3,484 metres. Much of the time the post can be enveloped in mist. Some of the Police Constables, finding life somewhat trying, sought some respite by going to the nearest purveyor of 'Millet Beer', a home-made brew that provides both nourishment and solace (homes in the mountains that sell home brew fly a white flag; some are rumoured to offer the traveller additional pleasures). It was dangerous to drink too heartily, as a wrong foot on the way back to post could involve a direct drop of 200 metres. Unfortunately, once or twice a year someone became befuddled both by the beer and the mist, and died a sudden death which, if nothing else, gave the Postings Clerk work to do.

The nearest small village is Mokhotlong ('the place of the bald ibis'), that sits at a comfortable 2,200 metres; even so the drop in temperature of an evening can be quite alarming. I stayed with the resident Ministry of Works (MOW) Inspector whose previous posting had been for several years in the Pacific Islands. When the Ministry of Overseas Development offered him a post in Africa, the Inspector was happy to accept the move providing the climate was tropical. He was assured that with an *average* day temperature of 20°C, he had nothing to fear. The Ministry official was probably unaware that during the night the temperature at altitude can drop to minus 12°C. Consequently I was greeted by a MOW inspector with one finger badly damaged by frost-bite.

Arriving in Botswana, one was immediately aware that the country is as flat as Lesotho is mountainous. The magnificence of the Kalahari Desert makes up two-thirds of a country that, whilst a little larger than France, has a population of about 1 million. In the north of the country the desert springs to life: the many thousands of square kilometres that make up the Okavango Delta or Swamp, formed by the river of the same name, which rises in Angola and forms in Botswana a vast network of lushly fringed waterways, before disappearing into the desert that surrounds the delta.

The inhabitants, the Tswana, are predominantly a pastoral society with cattle playing a major part in their lives. It is as impolite to ask a Tswana how many cattle he has as it is to ask his bank balance; for an answer to the former question would go a long way towards estimating the latter. In economic terms reference is made to the 'National Herd', although this does not indicate State ownership. During periods of drought, which are not infrequent and sometimes prolonged, the 'National Herd' can be reduced by several millions, due to the lack of both water and grazing.

Certainly a more peaceful population than that of Lesotho, the Tswana having lost a lot of their warrior instinct, the Government is truly democratic. As is common in most of the African States, the Special Branch or equivalent keep a watching brief on opposition political parties but no impediments are put in their path when elections are on.

Our house in Gaberone was set against the high brick wall of our illustrious neighbour Sir Seretse Khama, the President of Botswana. When adjusting the FM aerial on the roof of the bungalow, one had a clear view inside the grounds of State House and technically our kitchen fell within the prohibited area that Africans love to set up around the residence of the President. Sir Seretse was a good neighbour, a very pleasant man to deal with and he enjoyed the overwhelming support of his people. Whether discussing business on the phone or greeting me of an evening when out walking with his bodyguard of Special Branch officers trained in the latest bodyguard techniques by Superintendent Ray Tucker of the Metropolitan Police, Special Branch and ex-Kenya Police and I was out jogging, his demeanour was polite and the warmth of his smile pleasing.

Jenny had occasion one day to ring the local General Motors

agency, the Notwane Garage, to request assistance as our six-cylinder Chevrolet monster station-wagon refused to budge. Imagine her astonishment (after issuing directions, 'We live next to State House'), when Tshekedi Khama, one of Sir Seretse's twin sons, turned up to tow the car away. He was working as an apprentice mechanic and had now met his next door neighbours!

As Deputy Head of Special Branch stationed in Force Head-quarters at Gaberone, the day-to-day futility of monitoring opposition political parties was enlivened by the establishment of Eastern bloc Diplomatic Missions and events leading up to the independence of Rhodesia and the formation of Zimbabwe.

As many of my former Kenya Police colleagues were working in Rhodesia, I made a point of not visiting that country; neither did I take any part in conducting liaison meetings with Rhodesian Intelligence or for that matter, the South African services. One Rhodesian Special Branch officer, who met with my Botswana colleagues at a liaison meeting, visited Botswana on a clandestine mission late one evening a week or so later and was shot and wounded by a ZAPU guerrilla. It was unfortunate that when the Botswana Defence Force (BDF) followed up the incident the next day, the wounded Rhodesian was shot dead.

There were indeed parts of the dense bush straddling the Botswana–Rhodesian border that did sometimes harbour ZAPU or ZANU gangs (and at least on one occasion ANC guerillas bound for South Africa from the north), but they were not usually resident, merely transients escaping or regrouping from the rigours of armed clashes with the Rhodesian security forces, who sometimes crossed the Botswana border in pursuit of their quarry.

Incursions of the Rhodesian Light Infantry, or other units, in 'hot pursuit' was inevitably going to end in tragedy; and it was a sad day when my colleagues and I attended the funeral in Gaberone of some thirteen BDF soldiers who had been ambushed and killed by the Rhodesians, whilst travelling in Botswana in their BDF vehicles. There was an outcry against the Rhodesians for the unprovoked killing of the BDF soldiers;

in fairness, if that is the correct word, it has to be pointed out that the BDF patrol had actually picked up some armed ZAPU guerillas and were taking them back to camp. The Rhodesians regarded them as a legitimate target in the ruthless atmosphere of an armed struggle in which the ZAPU forces were already in command of large areas.

Far to the west on the Namibian border amongst the Kalahari sands, South West African People's Organization (SWAPO) gangs would sometimes seek the sanctity of a Botswana village inhabited by Bushmen. Also, as one would expect, South African security forces on anti-SWAPO patrols would also cross the border seeking out their foe. This area is sparsely populated, lacking water and virtually free from any resident authority. Reports pointed out that the South Africans were actually employing Botswana Bushmen, providing them with cash and clothing in an arid region where job opportunities were almost nil.

The enterprising South Africans were hiring the Bushmen on contract as trackers to hunt down the elusive SWAPO gangs and in the process they armed their recruits with automatic rifles. The local springbok had to watch out; this was a different ball game than being stalked by a bushman armed with a bow and arrow. They also provided them with ready access to alcohol. Local Bushmen lore has it that a contract tracker on leave from Namibia could be identified by his zig-zag spoor across the Kalahari desert.

In the Kalahari I met up with an American lady who was doing a survey for 'Voice of America'; she had a very plush four-wheel drive wagon and an attentive entourage. The lady was, however, completely thrown by local inhabitants, some Bushmen and the more prolific Kgalagari, whose favourite radio stations were first the BBC Foreign Service, then Radio Moscow and Peking. It was difficult for the American lady to believe that 'Voice of America' had no local clout. Listening to the BBC one evening, I felt the hairs on my neck bristle slightly as the newscaster was reading out a protest from the Botswana Government concerning the latest South African armed incursion. The details of the attack were very familiar, having been penned by me prior to my safari; and my askaris were impressed when I was able to tell them what was coming next.

Being a predominantly cattle country, Botswana works hard to combat foot-and-mouth disease, and progressive farmers were keen on vaccinations and keeping buffalo herds at bay. I once saw several Tswana men literally rolling on the floor with laughter after the wife of an American diplomat had told them (correctly) that cattle have hooves not feet and that the disease should be called hoof-and-mouth; she was serious and could not understand the mirth.

Being a newly-independent country, Botswana government officials were not always keen to take advice from western expatriates and, quite naturally, they wanted to be seen on some occasions to be 'non-aligned'. Against this background the police agreed to the secondment of several North Korean unarmed combat instructors; this in spite of the excesses of the infamous North Korean trained '4th Brigade' in Zimbabwe, which introduced a new element into subjugating one's own people. As any Special Branch views on the North Koreans were likely to be read as biased, the reporting was left to a local uniformed officer, who duly told his Commissioner of Police that the North Koreans were urging his Constables to defy their Commissioner, to query his orders and seek a more democratic police force in which they had the bulk of the say. The Commissioner eventually got the message; he took umbrage and the North Koreans left shortly afterwards for Pyongyang.

During the time of Rhodesia's Unofficial Declaration of Independence, there was an increase in the number of 'brass plates' that went up in Gaberone, as firms and individuals sought to trade with Rhodesia under the guise of local trade. In fact the only people they fooled were themselves, although actions against the culprits were rare as the magnanimity of the Botswana authorities and 'live and let live' seemed to prevail.

At a reception party thrown by Sir Seretse Khama on Botswana's National Day, I was standing alongside a large American businessman, amongst several hundred people in the grounds of State House, when he commented in a loud voice about the appalling security surrounding the President and how easy it would be for an assassin to strike. As I glanced at the President, I could see three members (armed) of his Special Branch bodyguard team, all unobtrusive – no ear-pieces! – one of whom had heard the visitor's remarks. Our eyes met and we smiled.

Cocktails at diplomatic receptions were invariably interest-ing and none more so than at the house of a Swedish diplomat, Joster Ronhedh. Joster was a great anglophile, indeed his wife, Barbara, was a former secretary to the Zanzibar Special Branch, where she told of her practice, when swimming, of placing the office keys in the waterproof confines of a product of the London Rubber Company which she hung round her neck.

As he handed me a drink in his lounge, Joster told me to move slightly to the right, where I would have clear sight of a large Swedish diplomatic envelope, complete with seals and classification, that he had placed innocently alongside the telephone as bait for the Soviet Ambassador Markov. The bait was not taken and, apart from the early departure of an ill British diplomat, the party ended quietly although for two of us there was an air of heightened anticipation throughout.

At the time of our acquaintance, Joster virtually drank no alcohol. In the past however he was apparently a lusty imbiber and great practical joker. In his study was the skin of a large Bengal tiger complete with head and green eyes. One day Joster summoned a servant to chastise him for some minor mis-demeanour and the servant fled in horror as the tiger rose from the floor and uttered a passable roar, after which Joster extracted himself from the skin and entered the 'noted blokes book' of diplomatic tales.

GLOSSARY

askari
East African soldier or policeman
baraza
meeting
barramills
water tanks (carried by camel)
boma
government offices (or a fenced enclosure)
braaivlais
barbecue (Afrikaans)
Bwana Bure
Mr Useless
bundu
the African bush
caracal
African lynx
chai
tea
chargul
canvas water-container
charubu
moustache
chinja
cut the throat
choma
burn
choo
lavatory

chuka
a sarong-like garment
dakki
underground hide (Kikuyu)
debbies
paraffin tins or jerry-cans
dhobi
washing
dia
'blood money' (Somali)
Dini Ya Msambwa
Religion of the Spirits of the Dead
donga
gully/dry riverbed
dubas
Somali tribal police
ferenji
European (Somali)
fid
conical wooden pin
gabdos
Somali maidens
geckos
house lizards
gerenuk
Wallers gazelle
ghat
a local stimulant
godown
warehouse or storeroom

gureis
Somali huts
herios
(camel) saddle-cum-mat
heshima
dignity or pride
inshallah
God willing
ilhumdillie
by the Grace of God
jilaal
the 'hot' season
kanga
guinea-fowl or vulterine
karai
cooking-pot
kariko
African tobacco
Kiama Kia Mwingi
Society of the People
kifaru
rhinoceros
kifuniko
cork or cover
kikoi
a sarong-like garment
Kinyanjui
a Kikuyu chief who was noted for
his statesmanship
kuni
firewood
kuru
waterbuck
kwale
Francolin partridge ('yellowneck')
lagh
seasonal river
lugga
dry water course
mabibi
women
machungwa
oranges/orange tree

makuti
coconut palm frond
manyatta
homestead of pastoral/nomadic
tribes
marifiki
friend
mbati
galvanised sheeting
mbogo (or nyati)
buffalo
mbutu
team or gang (Kikuyu)
michwa
white ants/termites
mkebe
tin
morani
warriors
mnyapara (neopara)
headman
mshenzi
barbarous
mswaki
a twig used as a toothbrush
mulla
holyman
murram
red laterine clay used for road
making
mzee
elder
mzigo
luggage
mzungu
whiteman or European
nabad gelyo
goodbye (Somali)
nabat
greetings (Somali)
nazerine
Christian (Somali)

ndeges
bird ('Crown Bird' cigarettes)
ngima
Sykes monkey
niatia
what is it? (Kikuyu)
njuri njeki
council of Meru tribesmen
neopara
native headman
nyati
buffalo
nyika
long-thorn acacia
panga
broad, heavy African bush knife
pombe
African-brewed beer
posho
ground corn flour
punda mavi
donkey's dung
rafiki
friend
Ramadan
Muslim month of fasting
rhakoub
camel section
Rinkals
spitting cobra
risasi
bullet
rondavel
round, grass-rooted hut
sangers
defensive positions

sime
African sword
shoats
collectively, sheep and goats
Shifta
cross-border raiders
shuka
loin-cloth
siafu
safari ant
silei
torture (Somali)
simama
halt
simba
lion
skellam
rogue (Afrikaans)
sufuria
saucepan
tumbo
stomach/belly
Vietmin
guerilla fighting French rule in
Indo-China
vlei
low-lying ground/clearing in
forest
waraba
hyena (Somali)
watoto
children
zariba
thorn-hedge or fortified camp
zebroids
a horse-zebra cross

INDEX

BIBLIOGRAPHY

Ian Henderson, GM, and Phillip Goodhart, 'The Hunt for Kimathi'. Western Printing Services Ltd, Bristol.

W. Robert Foran, 'The Kenya Police'. Clarke, Doble and Brendon Ltd, Plymouth.

Josiah Mwangi Kariuki, 'Mau Mau Detainee'. East African Publishing House, Nairobi.